# JUST GIV
# THE DAMN JOB!

# JUST GIVE ME THE DAMN JOB!

## HOW TO GET HIRED AFTER THE FIRST INTERVIEW

### A. LEE SMITH, PH.D.

Outskirts Press, Inc.
Denver, Colorado

The opinions expressed in this manuscript are solely the opinions of the author and do not represent the opinions or thoughts of the publisher. The author has represented and warranted full ownership and/or legal right to publish all the materials in this book.

JUST GIVE ME THE DAMN JOB!
How to get hired after the first interview
All Rights Reserved.
Copyright © 2011 A. Lee Smith, Ph.D.
v2.0

Cover Photo © 2011 JupiterImages Corporation. All rights reserved - used with permission.

This book may not be reproduced, transmitted, or stored in whole or in part by any means, including graphic, electronic, or mechanical without the express written consent of the publisher except in the case of brief quotations embodied in critical articles and reviews.

Outskirts Press, Inc.
http://www.outskirtspress.com

ISBN: 978-1-4327-7326-7

Outskirts Press and the "OP" logo are trademarks belonging to Outskirts Press, Inc.

PRINTED IN THE UNITED STATES OF AMERICA

# Just Give Me The Damn Job!
## How to get hired after the first interview

DON'T WASTE YOUR time studying 100 to 200 interview questions to nail the perfect job. It is more important to align one's physical and mental self into a synergistic force to become an interviewing powerhouse; this will prepare you to **answer whatever interview questions are thrown your way**. Once you read this book, you will know what it feels like to **take charge** of your next interview and **nail the job of your dreams**!

                              A. Lee Smith, Ph.D.

*DEDICATION*

*In memory of Terry Tench*
*Rest assured, TT, that we will never stop fighting*
*until there is a cure for amyotrophic lateral sclerosis.*

# Acknowledgements

I THANK MY family, friends and all of the contributors who supported my efforts and gave me loving advice for this book. Special thanks go out to my son, Keith, whose suggestions I sincerely cherished as I was putting the finishing touches on this vocation of pure joy.

# Table of Contents

Introduction ................................................................................ i
Chapter 1 – Knowing Thyself ...................................................... 1
Chapter 2 – Setting the Theme .................................................... 7
Chapter 3 – Knowing when to Hold and when to Fold ................ 17
Chapter 4 – Accepting the Job Offer before it's Offered .............. 21
Chapter 5 – How to Handle Inappropriate Interview Questions ... 25
Chapter 6 – Different Types of Interview Settings ....................... 29
    The Friend Interview ............................................................. 29
    The Dinner Interview ............................................................. 30
    The Multi Stage Interview ...................................................... 32
    The Telephone Interview ........................................................ 34
    The Video Conference Interview ............................................ 37
Chapter 7 – Defeating the Nerve Monster .................................. 39
Chapter 8 – What Hiring Managers are Looking For .................. 43
Chapter 9 – Dress Code for the Interview .................................. 47
Chapter 10 – Nail these Questions and You Nail the Job ............ 51
Chapter 11 – Conclusion ........................................................... 69
    Finding a job when you have a criminal record ..................... 69
    Aptitude and personality testing ............................................ 71
    Negotiating your starting pay ................................................ 73
    Thank you letters .................................................................. 75
Key Points to Remember ........................................................... 79

# Introduction

I'VE SPENT THE last 30 years in the business sector and in secondary education. During my tenure, I've interviewed for numerous jobs and interviewed hundreds of prospective candidates for a variety of employment opportunities.

The candidates that I've interviewed run the continuum, including that first job interview straight out of college, senior leadership positions, and the retiree who is looking to get back in the game. In fact, I was prepping Lloyd, one of those retirees, when he suggested I write this book. I'll get back to Lloyd a little later. Yet, what has become painfully clear to me about people interviewing for jobs is this:

**MOST PEOPLE DON'T HAVE A CLUE**
**HOW TO PREPARE FOR AN INTERVIEW**

Clueless! They may have the experience or the know-how. But, experience and know-how isn't enough if it can't be articulated to the person making the hiring decision. This doesn't mean that you aren't intelligent: it is saying that you have an inability to *SELL* your product-- and that product happens to be *YOU*.

Face it, at the top universities and colleges, there is no course in *HOW TO GET HIRED!* So, it's a little unfair to think that people will somehow master the interview just by showing up. So, I wrote this book to remove all of the guesswork out of preparing for the interview and getting the job.

As you read this book, feel free to jump around and grab what you need from here or there. Others will feel the need to read it from cover to cover in one sitting. How you decide to gather the information you need is totally up to you. If reading the book backwards hanging upside down from a chandelier gets you the job, then more power to you.

Oh yeah-- Lloyd. I met Lloyd during a camping trip in northwest Illinois. Lloyd is one of the reasons why I enjoy camping so much; you meet the most interesting people while out in the wilderness. As I was checking the water hookup to my RV, Lloyd stopped by my campsite to strike up a conversation, a common gesture in the world of camping. He was camping about sixty yards from where I had set up. As we started talking, Lloyd shared with me that he had been diagnosed with melanoma. As Lloyd described it, the cancer had surpassed the skin surface and started to invade healthy tissues. The doctors informed Lloyd that the progression of the cancer was fast, and they did not expect him to live for more than a year.

About the same time that Lloyd was receiving this not-so-pleasant news, his job was cutting back and offering its most senior employees buyout packages. Given the medical news, coupled with the thirty years that Lloyd put into the job, the buyout package looked like a pretty good deal. He took the deal, purchased a camper, and planned to travel America for as long as he could.

But Lloyd's very well-laid plan ran into a snag while he was down in Florida. During the course of one of his medical check-ups, his doctor told him that the treatments for the cancer were working, and they did not see why he wouldn't live a normal and, relatively speaking, healthy life. In other words, the family could stop planning his funeral because he wasn't going anywhere any time soon. Of course he was ecstatic, but he had one minor problem: he was out of work. And, since he was going to be hanging around awhile, he needed to find a job.

From April to October, Lloyd submitted resumes to seventy companies and he did get four interviews for his trouble. In fact, when I met him, he had an interview lined up that week at a local hospital in their Information Technology department. Lloyd had always worked in the engineering and computer science fields and believed that he would be a good fit for the job. Plus, he liked the fact that in the hospital's employment advertisement, it made note that older adults were encouraged to apply. Since Lloyd was 59, this seemed like a pretty good deal.

After listening to Lloyd's story, I wished him luck and told him that I would pray for him. I really wanted him to get that job. I went back to my camper and began to pray as promised. In the middle of my prayer, the question came to me: *I wonder if anyone has ever prepared Lloyd for an interview?* I wasn't going to get the answer in my RV, so I walked down the trail, knocked on Lloyd's RV door and invited myself in. "Hey Lloyd, when was the last time that you actually prepared for an interview - I mean going through a dry run with someone and receiving feedback?" His response was what I expected – "never." So, the next day, Lloyd and I spent two hours getting him prepared for his Friday morning interview. In working with Lloyd, there were some basic areas that I wanted him to understand so the interview experience would be pleasant and, most important, would make him the best candidate for the job.

I'll ask you what I asked him. *How well do you know yourself?* What is it about *you* that makes *you* the best person suited for this job? Second, it is critical to establish a theme for the interview. The theme is the thread that is consistent throughout the interview. It's the impression that the candidate wants to leave in the minds of the interviewer long after the interview is over. Third, the applicant must know when to expand on a response to a question and when to keep it brief. I call this the *knowing when to hold and knowing when to fold* strategy. Knowing when to hold and fold can only be achieved through preparation. Lastly, the applicant must let the interviewer know that he or she wants the job. I've interviewed many people

◄ JUST GIVE ME THE DAMN JOB!

over the years and, with some, I was never quite sure if they wanted the job or if they were practicing for some other job that they really, really wanted. Or, maybe they were using the interview opportunity to place pressure on their current employer for a promotion. If you want the interviewer to know unmistakably that you're interested in the position,

**DON'T LEAVE ANY DOUBT THAT YOU WANT THE JOB!**

After discussing my thoughts and ideas with Lloyd, it became clear to both of us that I needed to write this book to help others land that perfect job. In the next few chapters, I will discuss in more detail how to prepare for the interview through (1) knowing thyself, (2) setting a theme, (3) knowing when to hold and knowing when to fold and (4) understanding how to accept the job before it is offered.

CHAPTER 1

# Knowing Thyself

DURING MY YEARS of primarily consulting work, I was invited to tour the Franklin Lloyd Wright School of Architecture in Arizona. Franklin Lloyd Wright practiced the concept of organic architecture. Through organic architecture, everything evolves naturally through the inherent relationship between what is to be built, its surroundings, and the needs of the client. His structures are quite unique and are represented throughout the world. As I was taking this tour, the tour guide said something that helped me understand Franklin Lloyd Wright's philosophy of architecture. Wright believed that if one is to design a kitchen, they first must understand how to grow food. It took me awhile to make the connection. But, basically I understood Wright's philosophy to mean:

*BEFORE YOU CAN EMBARK UPON AN ADVENTURE,
IT IS FIRST NECESSARY TO UNDERSTAND ALL OF THE
DIMENSIONS ASSOCIATED WITH THAT ADVENTURE.
ONLY THEN CAN THERE BE ENLIGHTENMENT.
THAT ENLIGHTENED EXPERIENCE IS NECESSARY
TO CATAPULT YOU TO THE GREATER UNDERSTANDING
OF EXISTENCE AND PURPOSE.*

### JUST GIVE ME THE DAMN JOB!

This philosophy is germane to seeking employment as well. Nailing the job is the Holy Grail. But, nailing the job can't occur, won't occur, until certain learning and understanding takes place. Sure, it is important to know something about the job, but it is more important to know something about *You*.

Knowing thyself in context to the interview experience is equivalent to learning how to grow food to better understand how to design a kitchen. Knowing something about the job before stepping into the interview is helpful, but understanding *You* and how *You* are an indispensable and essential part of the process is paramount. Knowing thyself is the key to a greater understanding of the interview process. Knowing thyself is knowing ones' strengths and weaknesses and what makes *You* tick?

This is the point in the discussion where you must have that **conversation with yourself**:

- What am I good at?
- What is it about me that even drives me crazy?
- What are the parts of my personality that make me the dynamic person that I am or aspire to be?
- Where is it necessary for me to improve?

For now, I am not asking you to share this information with others, but it is a conversation that you must have with yourself first. Take me, for example. I know that I am a gifted speaker. I have a way of communicating with people that draws them in and leaves them wanting more. I'm good at it because I practice often and I enjoy the entire art of oration. On the other hand, I am not as good at dealing with specifics. I am great at envisioning the umbrella picture and motivating others to act. I like to lead in general terms and I rely on my managers to work out the details. I completed a personality profile test through Everything DiSC[1] and my score came back as an I.S. Through the Everything DiSC profile, people with an I.S. score are (**I**)nfluential, i.e., outgoing, enthusiastic, and optimistic;

---

[1] Everything DiSC © 2008 by Inscape Publishing, Inc.

## KNOWING THYSELF

and they are (**S**)teady, i.e., even-tempered, accommodating, and patient. My Myers-Briggs[2] personality trait is an ENTJ, which means I'm an (**E**)xtravert, I lead by (**I**)ntuition, I (**T**)hink through processes and I take on a (**J**)udging decision-making persona. Based on all of the profile tests that I have taken, it is apparent that I am outgoing, prefer to work in a collaborative fashion and I work to get the best out of people by making them feel valued. So, there – now, you have it. My strengths and weaknesses have been revealed for the entire world to see. I'm not asking you to reveal your most intimate secrets to others, but I do insist that you do so with yourself. *You must!* Only then can you be proactive and be in control of sharing and convincing others such as hiring managers and employment screeners.

***IT'S NOT JUST ABOUT SHARING, IT'S ABOUT CONVINCING THOSE WHO YOU WANT TO HIRE YOU THAT (1) YOU ARE WHO YOU SAY YOU SAY YOU ARE AND (2) YOU ARE MORE THAN CAPABLE OF FULFILLING THEIR JOB EXPECTATIONS.***

Before you can convince anyone about anything concerning you, you must first convince yourself. When I've applied for jobs and spoken about my strengths, it is clear to everyone in the room that I am who I say I am. It is me-- it is a part of me-- it is impossible for employers not to see. I am not only sharing my strengths in words, I am also convincing them at the same time through my actions, persona, and presence. I once went to a conference to hear Zig Ziglar speak, and he referred to his confidence this way: *"I'll go fishing for Moby Dick in a row boat and take the tartar sauce with me."*[3] Confidence is the key to convincing others you are who you say you are. Once you know what makes you tick, once you embrace the good, the bad, and the ugly, only then can you align your energies into a confident and concerted powerhouse which will be

---
2 Myers-Briggs & Co. Inc. - http://www.myersbriggs.com/
3 Zig Ziglar – Empowerment in the 21st Century, Cincinnati, Ohio Auditorium, 1988.

impossible for others to ignore.

Let's talk about weaknesses for a moment. You know – that part of our personality, work ethic, and business practice that we don't want anyone else to know. My friend shared a story with me concerning an employee whom he was interviewing for a regional management position. It was a situation in which the company was downsizing, management levels were being reduced, and managers had to interview for the same jobs within the company. As the employee engaged in the interview, the first thing that she revealed during the interview was that she didn't believe that she was qualified for the job, but she could learn and... WHO CARES WHAT ELSE SHE HAD TO SAY? I asked the only question that I could think of. Did she not want the job? Actually, she did want the job. It seemed, to my colleague anyway, that this was somehow a way of pointing out that she was a quick learner and that she would eventually rise to the challenge of the work. Maybe she would rise to the challenge, but there is one minor problem. She never got the job to find out. She wasn't hired because she placed on the record that she was not qualified.

If we take a deeper look at this, I see a couple of different sharks circling the proverbial water. I never spoke to this employee, but I wonder what sort of conversations she had with *thyself* before the interview? Did she truly understand her strengths and did she ever take the time to look in the mirror and articulate them? She might have been able to bring plenty to the job. Though it is true that there is no perfect employee, nor does there exist the perfect manager. It is essential to accentuate what you do very well and minimize the weaknesses by embracing them as part of your strengths. The problem or trap that most job-searchers fall for is attempting to segment themselves into opposite dimensions, i.e., good and bad, right and wrong, strengths and weaknesses. The problem with attempting to define *thyself* into these competing dimensions is the fact that God didn't construct us that way. Like it or not, we mere mortals are made up of multiple complexities that make us the unique individuals that we are. The latter point is critical to understand. Read it twice if necessary because it will prepare you for the dumbest of all interview questions – *what are your weaknesses?*

Basically, the interviewer is asking you to give up some information about your inner soul so he or she doesn't have to work to find it out on their own. And, what do interviewees typically do -- they spill their guts because they believe that they're doing the right thing, the just thing. What's really sad about it is that they are telling something negative about themselves that often isn't accurate. They embellish on a negative!

**AN INTERVIEW IS NOT A COUNSELING SESSION WITH YOUR THERAPIST. IT'S A JOB INTERVIEW IN WHICH YOUR RESPONSES TO QUESTIONS WILL MAKE OR BREAK YOUR CAREER.**

People become conditioned to respond to the *"what is your weakness"* question by thinking – well, I gave them something good, now I must give them something bad. Hey, is anybody home? The person interviewing you is not your therapist. It's an interview, it must be all good. GOT IT? The interview is not the time to reveal what you believe to be your most deplorable inner employment traits. Accentuate the positives and minimize the negatives.

Following is a sample of real applicant responses to real interview questions:

## What are your greatest weaknesses?

| Actual candidate response | How they should have responded |
|---|---|
| Well, I'm really not qualified to be a manager in the Injury Claims operation, but... | My ten years of insurance experience was primarily in the Property Damage Division where I developed my leadership skills. Although I don't have nearly the same experience managing an Injury Claims Division, I am confident that my leadership skills will serve me in that position as well. |
| I have a tendency to be unorganized in my work. But it is something that I am working on. | During my tenure as an office administrator, I've learned to appreciate the value of organization. Effective organization is an area that I have greatly improved in from the time that I started. |
| Typically, I'm not a morning person, so it takes me a little time to become engaged... | I often work late into the evenings because I find that as the day goes on, I do my best work. |

In each of the actual responses, the job applicant made the mistake of thinking that they were in therapy instead of an interview. Interviewers are human beings just like the rest of us. It is hard for them to get past the first thing that comes out of your mouth. When the applicant starts off with, I'm really not qualified, or I'm unorganized, or I'm not a morning person, it is difficult for the interviewer to hear anything else afterwards. Therefore, it is critical to accentuate the positive first, even when responding to a question that asks for a negative response. Remember, the first part of your response is what the interviewer will recall most vividly long after the interview is over.

CHAPTER 2

# Setting the Theme

HAVE YOU BEEN through interviews or do you know of interviews in which the company knows who they plan on hiring for the job prior to the job posting? Although such interviews can appear to be a waste of time, they still offer some value. First, the interview gets your name circulating among the hiring community. Second, there is no better practice than a real live interview. Third, and most important, you just might knock the socks off of the interviewer and require him or her to rethink their unofficial decision. This recently occurred for me. I was in the process of hiring faculty for a university for which I worked and was fairly certain who I wanted to oversee one of the business disciplines. However, I had already set up the last interview and it would have been discourteous to cancel, so I went through with it. Well, the candidate in the last interview made such an impression on the interview team, we offered him a position as well. The reason that they play the football game on Sunday, even though one team is clearly overmatched, is the same reason why it's important to follow through with the interview even when there is a strong inclination that some other candidate has the inside track.

*JOB CANDIDATES MUST FOCUS ON THOSE ACTIVITIES OVER WHICH THEY HAVE CONTROL*

Activities such as who has the inside track, or the rumor about Bob wanting to bring in someone from his golf foursome, or that Sara doesn't like to hire women are all things that you, the job applicant, have no control over. Plus, in many cases, the information is either completely wrong or half baked at best. Therefore the key for any job applicant is to prepare as well as possible for the interview and come out of the interview feeling good about your performance. Achieving your objective throughout the interview is what's most important.

Part of the interview preparation involves establishing a theme that you, the interview candidate, want to convey throughout the interview session. The theme is the dye-in-the-wool connection between you and the interviewer that is defined and totally controlled by you. As you think about the job for which you are applying, envision in your mind how you want the entire process to go – then, make it happen!

You will quickly learn that I like to use sports analogies when making comparisons. In this case, let's jump to basketball. The game of basketball has many great players, but there are only a few that were great jump shot artists. I'm not talking about the super whirlybird ball players who can leap out of the gym or are known for their ability to do a 360 degree slam dunk. I'm talking about the pure shooters. The players who took pride in the fact that they could consistently shoot the 15- to 22-foot jump shot with the greatest of ease and make it look like a lay-up. Every time the basketball was released from their hands, you held your breath because chances were, the ball was going to hit nothing but the bottom of the net. Jerry West may have been the greatest jump shot artist of all times. But there were others, including Andrew Tony of the Philadelphia 76ers, Larry Bird of the Boston Celtics, Ray Allen also a member of the Celtics and of course Oscar Robinson, the Big O who played with the Cincinnati Royals. With each of these great shooters, they had two things in common. First, they practiced for countless hours on shooting. Second, and most important, they envisioned the basketball going through the basket before ever releasing it from their hands. They had a mental picture

# SETTING THE THEME

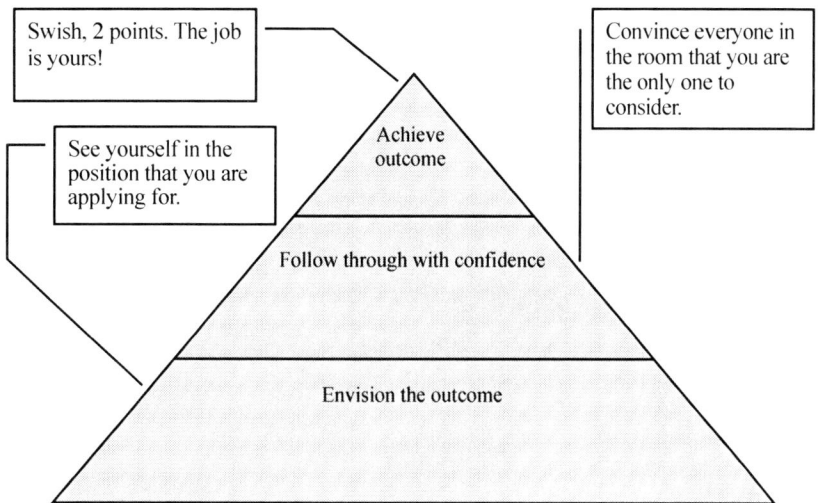

of the ball going through the hoop. They envisioned the outcome that they wanted and then they followed the script that resulted in the predicted outcome. The way West, Bird, Tony, Allen and Robinson thought about the art of shooting a basketball is exactly how job applicants must think about nailing the interview and getting the job.

Practice does make perfect. That garbage about over-preparing and making your responses appear canned is, well...garbage. If you lose a job opportunity because you were too prepared – live with it and move on to the next. Practice makes perfect. Think about what you want to project in the interview and what impressions you want to leave once the interview is over. Write these down. Then develop your interview strategy to achieve your projected outcome. This is your theme. It is unique to you and totally under your control.

You have a ready-made interview template to assist you for the interview prep. It's called the job advertisement. Most job advertisements list the job duties, functions, and required skills in a bullet list for easy and clear understanding. It just doesn't get any better or easier than this. As part of your interview prep, it is imperative for you to be able to speak to the job's expectations and how you will be able to meet those expectations. For example, a job advertisement for a real estate agent may contain the following information:

#### RESPONSIBILITIES INCLUDE

- The real estate agent is responsible for working with families to fulfill their dreams of buying and selling homes and commercial properties
- Negotiating contracts
- Communicating with banks, lenders, consumers and other essential parties of the property transaction process

#### QUALIFICATIONS

- Must have impeccable communication skills
- Valid driver's license
- Must know the geographical area
- Prior sales experience
- Thorough knowledge of MS Office products

As a job applicant for a real estate agent, the above information is your foundation for preparing for the interview. During your preparation, you want to be able to discuss how you are best qualified for the position by pairing your qualifications with the qualifications of the real estate position. Build this into your theme. Discuss your public speaking experience and give examples to demonstrate your communication skills. Be prepared to demonstrate your high level computer skills and how you were required to call on those skills in a prior job or situation. My point is, use the job advertisement to help develop your theme to present in the actual interview.

Another piece of information that is critical during the interview prep is your resume. The job screeners pulled your resume because it demonstrated that you had the fundamental attributes for the job. You put a lot of work in developing your resume and it earned you the interview. Now, you will use it to land the job. In preparing for

# SETTING THE THEME

the interview, be sure to go over your resume and know everything that's in it. You should be able to recite every job listed, explain every employment gap, and articulate each skill set that you've described in the resume. I assure you, during the interview, your resume will be front and center. Most likely, the interview team will have your resume with them as they are interviewing you. But, just in case they don't, bring extra copies with you to the interview. Some on the interview team will probably not have read it before the actual interview. However, they will expect you to know it as clearly as you know your own name. Knowing what's on your resume is a reasonable expectation. You wrote it; therefore you should know it. But, if you hesitate on a question pertaining to your own resume, it's a clear sign in the minds of the interview team that some of the resume information may be exaggerated. You never want members on the interview team to think that you are untruthful or that you are unethical. Thus, make sure that you can substantiate everything that is listed on your resume.

There is no perfect resume. There may be lengthy gabs between jobs, meager alignments between your skills and the job requirements, or the employment history may not be as strong as you would like. Such resume weaknesses are not showstoppers. They only present opportunities because you have taken the time to prepare. The key here is to anticipate the questions pertaining to these perceived resume weaknesses and prepare your response by turning the negatives into positives.

**THE RESUME GOT YOU TO THE INTERVIEW. BUT IT CAN ALSO LOSE YOU THE JOB IF YOU AREN'T ABLE TO DEFEND EVERYTHING THAT'S IN IT DURING THE ACTUAL INTERVIEW.**

Reviewing the company's website is a must in preparing for the interview. Give yourself adequate time to become familiar with the company by becoming familiar with their website. A great place to start is the section called, "About Us." Most company websites will have an "About Us" page or something similar to it. The information is usually general, but will guide you to other places to look for specific information. Know the mission statement of the company with which you are interviewing. You won't have to recite the mission statement during the interview, but it is great information to have in your hip pocket. Research the position for which you are interviewing. All of this research is valuable as it will help you prepare and anticipate the questions that you're most likely to receive during the interview.

Envision everything about the interview including your physical and emotional state. Clearly determine before stepping into the interview the theme that you want to project to the people interviewing you.

**THE INTERVIEW DOES NOT START WHEN YOU SIT DOWN TO RESPOND TO YOUR FIRST QUESTION, NOR DOES IT END AFTER YOU'VE ANSWERED THE FINAL QUESTION. IT STARTED THE SECOND YOU MET THE RECEPTIONIST IN THE LOBBY AND ENDED WHEN YOU WERE SAFELY BACK IN YOUR CAR DRIVING HOME.**

The word "theme" can be used as a noun, adjective or verb. For the following discussion, it will be referred to in its verb form and defined as "a unifying idea that is a recurrent element in literary or artistic work" (CMS)[4]. Unifying is the coming together, the act of uniting as one. So we are talking about uniting an idea in a recurrent framework, which is artistic in design, presentation and delivery. I don't want to diminish the theatric nuance of the term "theme" and how it is central to the interview process. In essence, the interview process is your opportunity to put on a show of great significance – an artistic show that excels in self confidence and preparedness, balanced with a touch of humility.

One prepares for the show, or in our case the interview, well in advance of entering the stage. The theme, that artistic universal presence, starts in the mind then envelopes everything else in a unifying

---
[4] **Chicago Manual Style (CMS):** theme. Dictionary.com. WordNet® 3.0. Princeton University. http://dictionary1.classic.reference.com/browse/theme (accessed: May 08, 2009).

presence. The theme is established in the mind, body, and overall appearance. Everything about you must be in lockstep with the theme. Your encounter with anyone you meet before or after the interview must be equally unified. You can't turn it on or off willy-nilly. The theme must be you, be inside you, and emanate from you every step of the way. When you go into that interview, there should be no mistake about it - the interviewer will know that you are who you say you are. The interviewer will know that what you say you can do-- you will do. Your theme is undeniably clear and you are believable to everyone in that room who is listening and taking it all in.

I spent a great deal of time with Lloyd helping him bring clarity to his theme. I actually prepared some notes for Lloyd following our interview preparation, which I have reproduced for this book. Refer to **Figure 1**.

# Figure 1

Hi Lloyd,

    As you prepare for your interview, think about the things that you want the employer to know about you. This is the theme that you want to convey. Here are some of the areas that I saw as your strengths. These you want to make sure that the hospital knows:

1. <u>You are customer service oriented:</u> Any person contacting you for assistance is your customer. This is the case whether they are an external customer or an internal customer. This must be part of your theme.
2. <u>You have strong intuitive skills as it relates to computer science:</u> You enjoy this work and you're good at it. You not only have a love for helping people with their IT concerns, you also have the skills to help them.
3. <u>You've stayed "fresh" and up to date in your knowledge of computer science and IT:</u> You've stayed young in the business by keeping up with the industry. You have continued your learning through different courses and through self help books. Plus, you are still familiar with many of the old programs that are often running in the background, but don't have a lot of IT support.
4. <u>You have a wealth of experience stemming from your education in engineering and mathematics:</u> You not only have the intuitive skills, but you were trained in the field. You have a strong math background that you transitioned into your love for computer science and IT.

    If asked the "tell me about your experience" question, focus on the last fifteen years. It's okay to start with the fact that you've received your initial engineering training through junior college, but leapfrog to your computer science / IT experience after that.

    Also, you want to be able to recite your strengths with relative ease. Try not to appear to be thinking of your strengths on the fly. As you shared with me, you have a:

(1) STRONG MATH BACKGROUND
(2) STRONG PROBLEM-SOLVING SKILLS
(3) SYSTEM MANAGEMENT EXPERIENCE
(4) A GREAT KNACK FOR DELIVERING EXCEPTIONAL CUSTOMER SERVICE BY ASSISTING PEOPLE IN A LANGUAGE THAT THEY UNDERSTAND.

****Important**** One of your best strengths is your ability to help people understand by speaking to them in <u>their</u> common language opposed to <u>your</u> "computer" language.

Don't ramble. Get to the point. Know what you want to say and move on. The best way to help you not to ramble is to prepare some basic responses to the most anticipated questions and practice, practice, practice.

Be able to tell your interviewers something about their company. When we spoke, you mentioned that you looked on their website and noted that J.D. Powers considered their hospital one of the best places to work. Tell them that! Interviewers like to know that you know something about the job for which you're interviewing. On Thursday, peruse their website and get a good feel for what the hospital is all about.

At the end of the formal interview, they will ask you if you have any questions. Have a few questions, but not too many. Keep it to two or three. <u>Also, let them know that you WANT THE JOB! Don't appear to be anxious, but leave no doubt that if offered the position, you will accept it.</u>

Tonight and Thursday, write down between six to ten questions and prepare answers for them. Practice, Practice, Practice. Most, important, GET A GOOD NIGHT'S SLEEP. It's hard to be at your best if you're tired.

Good luck, my friend!!!

Lee

CHAPTER **3**

# Knowing when to Hold and when to Fold

ALRIGHT, BACK TO the sports analogies. Boxing -- the sweet science. To non-boxing aficionadas, two men in the ring trying to punch each other to a bloody pulp is anything but sweet. Yet, for those who follow the sport, it is understood that the main objective is for one to hit the other while, at the same time, he avoids being hit. Avoiding that "being hit" part is easier said than done. In boxing, you will sometimes see one boxer simply overpower the other with shots to the head. The boxer will hit his opponent with a left hook to the head, rendering the unlucky chap groggy. Then, he hits him again to the head and this time, the punch literally wakes him up! Yeah, sort of strange, isn't it? The first punch knocks him onto Queer Street and the second punch actually helps him regain his equilibrium. There is a similarity between boxing and interviewing. Like the boxer who can become the victim of his own success, the interviewee can become the victim of the same sort of success by not knowing when to stop talking in response to an interview question.

During an interview, there are numerous dynamics at play. Of course, the interviewer is genuinely interested in the responses to their questions. If they weren't, they wouldn't ask them. But they are also just as interested in how the interviewee responds to the questions. They are sizing up body language, voice inflection, tone, style, response articulation, etc. Although you may have the right answers,

◄ **JUST GIVE ME THE DAMN JOB!**

you can still blow the interview if you don't pay attention to these tell-tale triggers.

One tell-tale sign that will shut down an interview quicker than a college frat party without beer is the rambling response. It's that interview response to a question that goes on and on, and on, and on, and on, and on. Rambling or not having a cutoff point in the response is a clear sign to the interviewer that you are making stuff up on the fly. Sometimes, rambling occurs when the interviewee is nervous. The interviewee may be prepared by doing the things that we've discussed earlier. But, he or she is overcome by nervousness and simply can't stop talking when it becomes natural to…ah, stop talking. It's like the boxer who may have rendered a good first punch, but loses his advantage because he does not know or understand that it is time to move on to a different strategy. From the interviewers' perspective, they don't care if the rambling is due to nervousness or being unprepared, they just want it to be over. Even worse than ramblers are the self-indulgent types who have done it all; they're a legend in their own mind. You need to be careful here. Yes, the interview is your time to shine. It's your time to get to know the company and for the company to get to know you. But it is possible to go overboard and drag the interview into a self-indulgent summation that rarely results in appropriate responses to what is being asked. I was conducting an interview with an applicant who was applying for a research professor position. The interview was only supposed to last an hour. This one lasted two and a half hours. He just wouldn't shut up! We would ask the interviewee a question about his experience as a research professor and he would respond with a discussion about his interviews with world leaders from the Middle East. It simply became a bizarre situation. Oh, we also learned that he had a photogenic memory, reads 2,000 words a minute, was the architect of a major news organization and he might have played three different professional sports. When I told him that he didn't get the job and why, he couldn't believe it. His surprise didn't surprise me, given the fact that I already knew he thought he was the Second Coming of Jesus Christ.

# KNOWING WHEN TO HOLD AND WHEN TO FOLD

***IT IS IMPORTANT TO <u>SELL YOURSELF</u>, BUT ALSO MAKE SURE TO <u>CHECK YOURSELF</u> SO YOU DO NOT COME ACROSS LIKE A SELF-ABSORBED KNOW-IT-ALL***

Balancing between when to *HOLD* by continuing the dialogue and when to *FOLD* by wrapping it up can be readily handled by following a few simple rules:

Practice, practice, practice: If you think that you've heard this advice before you are correct. Practicing days before and the evening before the interview helps to calm your nerves. Practice prepares you for what's to come. And, when you are prepared, you are less likely to be nervous. When you aren't nervous, you are much less likely to ramble. Practice leads to confidence – confidence in your belief that you are prepared to answer any question that comes your way.

Anticipate the questions and be ready to respond to each individually: This could have been part of the Practice rule, but it is so important, I wanted it to stand on its own. You may not know the exact questions that will be asked, but you can anticipate the types of questions based on the type of job. In addition, there are basic questions that are asked in every interview. I have devoted an entire chapter to the basic interview questions, which will come up later in this book. If you nail the questions, you nail the job.

Hear yourself speak: During the interview, it's easy to get on a roll. Before you know it, you're firing off answers to questions but really not listening to your own words. You are on auto pilot. Being on auto pilot is a good thing if you are flying a jumbo jet, but during an interview, you need to be mindful and attentive of your own words. Only then can you take control of what you're saying. If you feel that you're talking too much, and the glazed eyes of the interviewers confirm your suspicion, wrap it up.

Answer the question first – What I find troubling in some interviews is when the applicant renders a long, rambling response to a question, but never answers the question posed by the interviewer. This is seen by the interview team as a stall tactic – the applicant doesn't know the answer and is hoping if enough junk is slung against the wall, they'll buy it. To avoid this scenario, simply answer the question first, before you start explaining the how, when, and what. For example, if the question is, "Please explain how you improved your operation in your last position," the response should start off with something like, "I improved my operation by…" After stating two or three ways the operation was improved, then give the details of each while being mindful and attentive of your words.

CHAPTER **4**

# Accepting the Job Offer before it's Offered

YOU HAVE COME too far to let the job slip away now. Last night after dinner, you went over all of your interview notes. You got up this morning and put on your best suit, which just arrived from the cleaners. You are looking so sharp that you could cut cheese with your sleeves. The interviews start at 8:00 a.m. and the last interview wraps up around noon.

The interviews are almost over and you have been fantastic up to this point. The interview team has no more questions for you and you're in the process of asking your final questions. Everyone is about to leave. You may be going back home or back to that job from which you want to resign. The interview team has to get back to their desks because they've just spent the morning with you and their emails are piling up as well. **Wait!**

**DON'T YOU DARE LEAVE THAT INTERVIEW WITHOUT LETTING THEM KNOW THAT YOU WANT THE JOB!**

Have you ever gone to a movie that had one of those new age endings that didn't tie up the loose ends? As the lights flick on in the theater and the credits started to roll, the audience has this peculiar expression on their faces, as if to say, *That's it?* For some interview wrap ups, it's like that movie with the *what-the-heck-just-happened* ending. You may have done well throughout the entire interview, but now it's done, and the interviewers just aren't sure if you really want the job. There's an easy way to make sure that you don't leave any doubt in the minds of the people who are making the hiring decision – you must tell them that you want it!

It's truly that simple. Don't leave them guessing like the ending of some new age movie. Make sure that they're crystal clear in their understanding that you want to start working as soon as possible.

I recall interviewing for a mid-level management position in Florida quite a few years back. I was already working for the same company in Ohio, but the Florida job was going to be a nice promotion, and I would be making a great deal more money. Oh yeah, I wanted the job. The interview went along as expected. I was placed at the head of the table in the executive conference room. Leadership from all departments was present. I wasn't nervous because (1) I had prepared for the interview, (2) I had already envisioned myself in the new position, (3) my confidence was present throughout the conference room, and (4) I looked, felt and acted the part of the person who was already selected for the position. In other words, I put into action all of the things that we have covered in the previous pages of this book. I was feeling good. Heck, I was good and everyone knew it in that conference room. I was not cocky; I was simply confident. As the interview was wrapping up, I asked the few questions that I had already prepared. Then, I thanked them all for the interview and I left them with this:

*"Again, I want to thank you for this opportunity and I want you to know that I am more interested in this job today than I was before having had the chance to speak with each of you. And, if I am your final selection for the position, I am ready to start work as soon as you and my Ohio management team can work it out."*

If there was any doubt in the minds of that interview team whether or not I wanted the job, I just erased it. In addition, I doubt if the other candidates made it as crystal clear as I did regarding their interest in the job. So, if the decision was between me and someone else, they were probably going to select the candidate who demonstrated the strongest desire for the position. Now, if you have to think about it because you have other commitments such as another job offer pending, or there's something that won't allow you to commit just then – well, that's a different story. It wouldn't be ethical to string the group along by stating that you are ready to start working when in actuality, you aren't. But, if you are ready to go, make sure you don't leave any doubt on the table. Also, by letting the group clearly know that you want the job, and that you are ready to start working, demonstrates decisiveness, which is always a positive virtue to present in an interview setting. As we are discussing the virtues of decisiveness, confidence, etc., understand that these attributes must be part of the larger framework that includes preparation and knowing thyself. And, yes, I got the position.

CHAPTER 5

# How to Handle Inappropriate Interview Questions

OVER THE LAST twenty years, I've seen a significant improvement in the composition of interview teams and in the questions that they ask during the interview process. In most cases, teams assembled to hire the best candidate for the job know what they're doing. They are asking the right questions and, in most cases, they are smart enough to assemble following the interview, discuss pros and cons, and come to a joint decision as to whether to hire a particular individual. I think companies do a disservice to themselves as well as the applicant when only one person conducts the interview and makes the hiring decision. When the interview process involves only one lone soldier, employers run the risk of creating an organizational culture that lacks diversity, which never ends up being a good thing.

Human Resource departments are the primary reason why the interview process has improved over time. HR teams often develop a set of questions for each position and require that each candidate be asked the same set of questions. Asking each candidate the same set of questions ensures that the interview team is measuring apples to apples and it prevents the rogue interviewer from going off on his or her personal crusade, which may have nothing to do with the job opening. The increase in lawsuits filed by job applicants against companies with claims of discrimination has also played a huge role in the improvement of the interview process. Companies have learned quickly that interview questions must pertain to ones' ability to perform the essential or key functions of the job, period. In other words, interview questions should only be asked of an applicant that will determine his or her ability to perform in the job for which he or she is interviewing. Although some interviewers still do, they aren't supposed to ask job applicants if they plan on getting pregnant within the next year. Although some interviewers still do, they cannot ask job applicants if they are married, or how many children they have, or what religion they practice, or the profession of their spouse. If these types of questions don't pertain to the essential functions of the job, then it is inappropriate to ask them and, in some states, it is illegal to pursue such lines of questioning altogether.

Unfortunately, I have been on interview teams in which the participants never should have been allowed anywhere near an interview session. I've heard all of the questions to which I just alluded. I've also been the interviewee where oddball questions were thrown my way. In one particular situation, I was interviewing for a management position. I had already worked for the company in a non-managerial role, so the two individuals knew me from my previous work. This happened to be a dinner interview. One of the people interviewing me was the assistant vice president and the other was the regional manager. We will call the regional manager, Ralph in this case. And the drinks were flowing. The particular question that I will discuss here came from Ralph after three double scotches. By the way, I'm going to discuss difficult interview situations later, and you better believe, the dinner interview is one of them. So, well into the evening, Ralph asked me something that went sort of like this,

*"You know, Lee. If we hire you for the position, there are going to be a few people who believe that the only reason that we hired you is because you are black. What do you think about that and how do you plan to demonstrate in the job that we didn't hire you just because you're black?"*

## HOW TO HANDLE INAPPROPRIATE INTERVIEW QUESTIONS ➤

I follow a personal motto of not drinking during interviews whether I'm interviewing someone else or if I'm being interviewed. It is at times like this that I am so glad I follow my own non-drinking policy. I honestly don't think that the regional manager would have asked me such an inappropriate question if his belly (and brain) had not been filled with three double scotches on the rocks. And, I probably would still be regretting that evening if I'd followed their lead of alcohol consumption, if just for that one dinner. But, here we were. The question was posed and they were waiting for an answer. My response went something like this:

*"I plan to do nothing to convince my coworkers, superiors, or those who work for me that I was promoted for any other reason besides my being the best candidate for the position. The question you raise is not my problem, it's theirs. My job is to do the job that you've promoted me to do. Now, if the issue affects productivity in my operation, then we will have to address the matter based on the facts, circumstances and the conditions associated with the performance."*

I will bet you a plum nickel that no one else applying for the position got that ridiculous question. They couldn't have since I knew that the other candidates were all white. I guess that I had many options before me in responding to Ralph's interview question. I could have told him that it was an inappropriate question, which I wouldn't dignify with an answer. I could have replied with a response that reflected my annoyance with the question. But, I didn't do that either. You see, I wanted the job. And I felt pretty good about my response. Although I didn't prepare for such a question, my overall preparation gave me the confidence to be prepared for the unknown, the unfamiliar, and, in this case, the inexcusable.

During the interview, if you are asked an inappropriate question, you will have to decide for yourself how to respond. You can answer the question – and, if offered the position, decide if the organization's culture is something of which you want to be a part. Unless the question is too outrageous and over the top, my recommendation is: (1) keep your cool, (2) don't show your agitation, and (3) answer the question, while maintaining your professionalism and dignity. Following the interview, make sure that you write down the question or questions that were asked, along with your responses, for safe keeping. If offered the position, then decide if this is a place where you want to work. If not offered the position, I strongly suggest that you think about whether discrimination may have played a part in the decision and report the incident to your local U.S. Equal Employment Opportunity Commission (EEOC). The EEOC is the branch of the Federal Government that serves as watchdog over unfair employment practices. You've worked too hard to get to where you are. You should never allow discrimination practices to prevent you from achieving the career aspirations to which your hard work has entitled you.

CHAPTER 6

# Different Types of Interview Settings

DEPENDING ON THE job and the company, the interview setting can vary significantly. The interview may be extremely informal-- the setting, literally a walk in the park with you and the person who may hire you. On the other hand, the interview can be quite formal and cover more than a day of discussion. The size of the company will play a part in how formal or informal the interview will be. The pendulum of the interview setting offers too wide an arc to address them all. So we will touch on a few situations that you are most likely to encounter or that may cause the highest degree of angst. The interview settings that we will discuss are: (1) the friend interview, (2) the dinner interview, (3) the multi-stage interview, (4) the telephone interview, (5) and the video conference interview.

## The Friend Interview

Be afraid. Be very afraid of the "Friend Interview." This is simply a situation where your good friend is conducting the interview. First of all, it's great that you have the right connections to be interviewed by someone to whom you are close. That is what networking is all about. What could go wrong? He or she is your friend for goodness sakes. Actually, the friend interview is one of the trickiest interviews through which you'll sit. There is a tendency to think that since this is your friend, there is less of a need to prepare in the same way one would when interviewing with an unknown group. You are inclined to think that you already have the job just because old buddy Bob is conducting the interview. Keep in mind that old buddy Bob has others to answer to for his performance. Thus, if you get the job and don't perform, Bob's job is on the hook and he knows it. So, Bob may have gotten his friend the opportunity of a lifetime; but it is still up to you to demonstrate that you are the best candidate for the job. Therefore, you should prepare for the friend interview just like you would prepare for any other interview. Don't leave any doubt that you are the best candidate for the job. Plus, you owe it to your friend to put your best foot forward. If he or she pulled strings to get you the opportunity, you owe them the best that you have to offer.

## The Dinner Interview

So you think that you made it. The company was impressed with your resume. They even picked up the tab to fly you in from the town of who-knows-where to interview for the job of who-knows-what. You have to be feeling pretty good right about now. Better yet, the interview is taking place over dinner at the nicest restaurant in town. Come on, it can't get any better than this. You must be thinking that you already have the job and this dinner interview is just a formality. Well, think again! The dinner interview is anything but a slam dunk. In fact, you can lose the opportunity of a lifetime if this talk over prime rib is not handled just right.

There are many reasons why an employer would want to take you out to dinner as part of the interview process. The most obvious reason is to see how you act in public. If, for example, part of your job is to entertain clients or sell high-end products, it is important to have an outgoing personality and a professional demeanor. One may be able to pull the wool over the interviewer's eyes in a one-hour office interview. But it is difficult to fake the real you over a two-hour dinner. The dinner interview setting is a more candid environment.

## DIFFERENT TYPES OF INTERVIEW SETTINGS

It is not uncommon for a job applicant to respond to questions differently during a dinner interview than he or she would in an office room setting. Nor is it unlikely for the interviewer to ask different sorts of questions or hold a different type of discussion during dinner than he or she would with you at the office. In other words, the gloves are off, and your ability to navigate through this unstructured interview environment is a critical step in determining whether or not you land the job. Understand that:

### *THE DINNER INTERVIEW HAS NOTHING TO DO WITH DINNER!*

It's an interview, which is no different than any other type of interview. This is not the time to be uptight. Nor is it the time to let down your guard.

- Be yourself
- Be prepared
- Be professional
- Be smart
- Be cool

I've already shared with you my concerns about drinking during an interview. I'm not here to tell you what to do. But I will give you a few things to think about. I am simply not at my best doing anything after I have had a few drinks. And yes, I personally know people who perform quite well in certain situations only after they have had a few drinks. So for me, I will never drink alcoholic beverages during an interview. Not because it's the right thing to do, but because I just don't want to fall out of my chair or slur the name of the person that I am hoping will hire me. But what if you are interviewing for a job in which you are required to entertain people and drinking is part of the culture? In such a case, having a drink or two is perfectly acceptable if you and the interview team are comfortable with doing so. I would not suggest drinking during an interview if your only reason for doing so is to impress someone else. Also, it's always a good idea to defer to the interview team to make the first move. Imagine the waiter coming to your table and asking would anyone like to start off with a cocktail and you jump at the chance to order your double martini only to be followed by the members of the interview team ordering iced tea and colas. Yeah, you don't want to be caught in that position. So, in summary, be sure that you understand the organizational culture and that you make a wise decision based on everything you know about the situation. Regardless of your decision to drink or not to drink, it is NEVER a good idea to over indulge and be taken off of the strong game that you have worked so hard to prepare.

## The Multi-stage Interview

The multi-stage interview usually takes place in a very formal setting. The company is probably large, with a complex organizational structure. The interview may encompass a few days and is always preceded with an interview schedule letting the candidates know who they will interview with and when. Let's say you are interviewing for a client-based marketing position. The interview schedule may look something like I've prepared in **Figure 2**:

# Figure 2

Interview Schedule for Mr. Bob Saunders

**Monday**
| | |
|---|---|
| 7:30 a.m. | Breakfast at hotel with Jim Phillips, marketing manager |
| 8:30 | Valerie Smith, human resources manager |
| 10:00 | Helen Davis, marketing analyst |
| | Shaun Williams, research analyst |
| 11:00 | Grace Webb, accounting supervisor |
| Noon Lunch | Helen Davis and Shaun Williams |
| 2:00 p.m. | Keith Smith, director of Operations |
| 3:00 | Visit with marketing team |
| 6:00 | Dinner |

**Tuesday**

| | |
|---|---|
| 8:00 a.m. | Albert Little, marketing assistant vice president |
| 9:00 | Juan McVeigh, supervisor of information technology |
| 10:30 | Jim Phillips will fly Mr. Saunders back to the airport |

The multi-stage interview, as depicted in Figure 2 can appear intimidating on its surface. In actuality, this interview is where you can turn lemons into lemonade. In the job candidate role, I have always found the multi-stage interview to be an environment in which I did my best. First, it is great to know in advance the names and titles of the people on the interview team. This information is golden. If they did not provide the names to you, ask the hiring manager's assistant for the information. Once you have the names, you can Google them or look them up on any number of social networking sites to gather intelligence that just may be useful during the interview. Doing such research is not inappropriate. This is part of preparing for the interview.

### *REMEMBER, YOUR JOB IS TO GET THE JOB AND DO SO BY ANY ETHICAL MEANS NECESSARY.*

If, for example, you learn that Albert Little, AVP of marketing studied theater at Harvard University or is an officer of the American Marketing Association, such information may come in handy during your discussions with him. I was recently helping a friend to prepare for his interview and he told me that during his research, he learned that the he and the hiring manager went to the same out-of-state high school. During a break in the interview, the high school connection came up in conversation and appeared to have been one of the points that may have influenced the manager's decision to hire him. Caution! Don't force it into the conversation, but have it as background to help you guide the conversation in a positive direction. It's all about preparation.

What's also nice about the multi-stage interview is the fact that the information that you are provided in the morning is the same information that you can use in the afternoon to emphasize a critical point. I was interviewing for a job in a multi-stage setting and the entire morning was spent basically telling me what the plans were for the organization moving forward. I was provided information regarding what senior leadership envisioned in each department, the challenges of the organization and of the industry. It was great stuff. I couldn't have researched this specific information if I had tried. Sure enough, when I got into the afternoon sessions, one of the first questions posed to me was to list the areas upon which I would focus during my first six months on the job. Hey, my momma didn't raise a fool. I fed them the exact information which I had just learned that morning. Such luck can only happen in a multi-stage interview.

Not all multi-stage interviews start off with breakfast. Most, however, include dinner with members of the interview team if the interview extends to more than a day. If breakfast is included, the same rules as the dinner interview apply. Usually, the breakfast interview consists of information for how the day is going to proceed. It also serves as an icebreaker for the individuals to get to know each other. I like it when the interview starts with breakfast because it usually calms the nerves and gets the applicant ready for a long, and what will be a very exciting, day.

## The Telephone Interview

Telephone interviews usually take place during the vetting stage. It is a quick and easy way for the interviewer (or screener) to determine if there is any need to take the applicant further in the interview process. This is the company's opportunity to see if there is a possible fit and, if there is, a more formal interview will follow. The telephone interview is fast paced and takes on a just-the-facts tone. Most likely, the phone interview will be conducted by a human resources representative who is trying to whittle down the stack to get to the top three or four candidates to call in for a more comprehensive screening. She or he will have your resume in front of them while they are talking to you and will simply go down the list of your accomplishments while

## DIFFERENT TYPES OF INTERVIEW SETTINGS

asking you to respond to each.

Obviously, if you don't get through the telephone interview, you have zero chance of being called back for the more formal interview. You must prepare for the telephone interview in the same manner that you would for the in-person interview. If the interview is at 8:00 a.m., don't roll out of bed at 7:45 with the thought that this phone interview doesn't require planning or practice. Just like any other interview, preparation is the key. So, get up and get dressed. If you are calling from home, make sure that you won't be interrupted by friends and/or family. Let your family know in advance that you will be on a phone call and can't be disturbed for the next thirty minutes. Have your information, (i.e. notes, screen shots, resume) available and positioned where you will not have to shuffle a lot of paper while on the call.

There are a couple of ways to ensure that you do your best during the phone interview. First, know who's calling who. If you are in a different time zone than that of the interviewer, be sure to verify the correct time of the call. These clarifications may seem trivial, but if they're expecting you, the applicant, to initiate the call, but you are waiting for the interviewer to call you, chances are that you've blown the interview before it ever gets started. The same goes for time zone misunderstandings. Doesn't make any difference who blew the time, it's your fault and you most likely won't get the job as a result. Take the thirty seconds necessary to confirm who is initiating the call and to clarify the time zone issue if appropriate. Next, know everything that is on your resume and be able to respond to questions regarding your experiences. This is a good rule for any type of interview, but it is most important here because this is a screening interview and you are going to be quizzed on it during the call. Don't try to read off of your resume in responding to questions posed by the interviewer. You may be tempted to do so because it's a phone interview and you're thinking that since they can't see you, they won't know. Trust me on this one – even an untrained screener can pick up very quickly over the phone when someone is reading from a script. It is an immediate turnoff and you will most likely never hear from the company again.

### JUST GIVE ME THE DAMN JOB!

I had a funny incident take place during a phone interview. A couple of colleagues and I were conducting some initial screenings for a professorship position. As we were asking our questions, we could hear someone else, not the applicant, in the background telling the applicant what to say in response to the question. It was the strangest interview situation I've ever experienced. We would ask a question and after each question, there was a pause and, eventually, the applicant would come back online with a response. It became so obvious that we finally had to ask the applicant if there was someone else in the room. He denied it, but it was pretty clear, at least to us, what he was doing. Actually, I thought the person who was truly providing the answers did a pretty good job. Maybe we should have considered the friend instead of the person we set up for the interview.

Make sure that you have a clear and uninterrupted phone signal for the telephone interview. Nothing is more irritating than hearing twenty minutes of phone static while trying to conduct an interview. If you know, and you should know, that your phone has a poor connection, don't use it. Make arrangements for the call to be conducted on a telephone with a clear signal. Landlines work better than cell phones. If possible, don't use a cell phone for the phone interview. And, if you are forced to use a cell phone, make sure that you have enough battery life to get you through the call. It is frustrating for everyone when the applicant's cell phone goes dead during the call or he or she has to stop the interview to change phones, change batteries, or whatever to continue the call. During the interview, you want to demonstrate that you are a prepared individual. Phones going dead or phones with poor connections during the call can only speak to your unpreparedness. Lastly, know how you sound on the telephone. And, don't think that you already know without hearing yourself from outside yourself. Have you ever listened to your own voice through a tape recorder? The tape recorded voice sounds nothing like the real you to you. But it's what other people who know you are accustomed to hearing every time they interact with you. Do a mock interview on the phone with a friend and ask for feedback. Or, answer the interview questions that

DIFFERENT TYPES OF INTERVIEW SETTINGS

you've prepared into a tape recorder so you can hear firsthand how you sound. Because it is a telephone interview, you don't have any of the body language communication to help you make your point. All you have is your voice and its various inflections. So, know how you sound to others on the phone and eliminate all distractions and noise by using an unobstructed phone system.

## The Video Conference Interview

Technology has finally caught up with the pace of business. Nowhere is this more apparent than in the area of webcasting. I have very few employees who share the same building space as I do. But I can still communicate with them as if our offices were side-by-side. There are numerous webcasting devices currently on the market. Personal computer performance is 100 times better today than it was just five years ago. As a result, video interviews can now be conducted with just a high-speed PC and a video cam. More companies are taking advantage of this technology for obvious reasons. It's cheap. Why fly an applicant halfway across the country when, in fact, you can simply interview them over the web?

Interviewing a job candidate using a video cam connected to a PC is the most basic form of using the video technology. But, for a reasonable cost, the employer can conduct the interview by having the candidate visit a growing number of locations that will rent webcasting time and space for meetings and for interviews. Employers may want to hold a video interview opposed to a telephone interview mainly so they can see the potential employee. The video interview takes on the atmosphere of a face-to-face encounter. In actuality, it is face-to-face; the only difference is that the interviewer and the interviewee are separated by distance. Therefore, if you are being interviewed by live video, you must treat it exactly the same way as you would a face-to-face interview.

Unlike the telephone interview, the video conference interview is more formal and will most likely be conducted by the hiring manager, not the HR representative. The hiring manager will usually be flanked by other department heads and/or unit managers during the interview.

The video conference interview, also called a web conference interview, is a nice forum for such a meeting – that is, if all of the technology goes as planned. How many times have you watched the evening news or one of the morning news talk shows and the video feed malfunctions? It happens quite often if you think about it. When watching the news, you've heard the phrase before, *"Okay, we've just lost our feed from Seattle. We'll pick right back up with Mike on the other side of break. Take it away, Jane."* The national evening news and the morning talk show broadcasts have some of the most sophisticated communication systems in the world. Yet, they still break down. So, if it can happen to Matt Laurer hosting the Today Show, you bet your bottom dollar that a technical glitch can happen to you when you're interviewing for the job of a lifetime.

### *THE FIRST DEFENSE THAT YOU HAVE AGAINST TECHNICAL GLITCHES IS PREVENTION. KNOW YOUR EQUIPMENT!*

If you are going to use your own PC and video cam equipment, test it out first. Make sure that the location is free from distractions (i.e., family members, barking dogs, noisy neighbors) and that you have a clear transmission signal. If you are conducting the video interview at a professional site, chances are that the company is paying for it and may, in fact, select the location. Nevertheless, test it out first. Go to the location where the video interview is to take place. Ask the technician to set it up for you and have him or her demonstrate its functionality. This may seem like a lot to go through, but doing so can make the difference between success and failure. If a technical glitch does occur during the interview, don't panic. You aren't the first and you won't be the last for which such mishaps have occurred. Stay cool, work through the problem, and continue, once the issue is fixed. Remember, how you conduct yourself in a crisis situation says a great deal about you in the minds of the interview team.

CHAPTER 7

# Defeating the Nerve Monster

THERE IS NO one that I've met that has not been attacked at some point in their life by the nerve monster. The nerve monster is that intolerable creature that seeps into your nervous system at the most inopportune time with the sole purpose of making you sweat, raising the pitch of your voice, preventing your flow of oxygen to the lungs and taking you off of your well prepared game plan.

The nerve monster loves to show up at interviews – this is where he does his best work. The setting may already be tense, and there is a lot riding on your performance. You better believe that the nerve monster is lurking. This may surprise you, but we don't want to slay the nerve monster. We just want to control him so you can be at your very best during the interview. In fact, you will actually need him in order to reach your peak performance.

That feeling of nervousness, which comes on right before preparing for a major event, is a form of energy. Positive energy is needed for you to perform at your very best.

**YOU DON'T WANT TO SUPPRESS NERVOUS ENERGY.
YOU WANT TO EMBRACE IT AND USE IT
TO YOUR ADVANTAGE.**

We all have experienced some form of nervous energy when

preparing to do something that is very important to us. Although the triggers are different for each of us, no one is immune from nervous energy or potentially, immune from the nerve monster. When I prepare for a lecture that I will present to my colleagues, I feel that energy throughout my entire body. But, to avoid being overcome by the nerve monster, I am able to turn that nervousness into positive energy and use it to my advantage. Again, it is not our intent to slay the nerve monster. We want to control and use it to our advantage. The nerve monster can turn from foe to friend through appropriate preparations.

Preparation is where you can use that stored up positive energy to your advantage. Using that energy to make sure you are on top of your game is essential and carrying it into the interview is critical. Know thyself, establish your theme, study the job and be ready to sell yourself during the interview. Once you have adequately prepared for the interview, you won't be concerned about being nervous. You'll be eager for the opportunity to strut your stuff. This is when the interview actually becomes fun. The interview team will pick up on your excitement, which in part is due to the positive energy that you are carrying along with you. Preparation is the key to taming the nerve monster and turning him from foe to friend.

Next, and equally important is making sure that you get enough sleep the night before the interview. In fact, getting enough rest is something that should be a habit. You may recall in the early part of this book the note that I wrote to Lloyd in which I told him to get a good night's sleep before the day of the interview. Getting a full night's rest is also essential for controlling your nervous energy during the interview. David F. Dinges, Ph.D., is a psychologist and sleep expert of the Division of Sleep and Chronobiology and instructor in the Department of Psychiatry at the University Of Pennsylvania School Of Medicine. He states:[5]

> Irritability, moodiness and disinhibition [sic] are some of the first signs a person experiences from lack of

---
5 Dinges, Sleep, Sleepiness and Performance, 1991

sleep. If a sleep-deprived person doesn't sleep after the initial signs, said Dinges, the person may then start to experience apathy, slowed speech and flattened emotional responses, impaired memory and an inability to be novel or multitask.[5]

To function at your best during the interview, you must have enough sleep the night before. The last thing that you want to exhibit during the interview is the signs that Dr. Dinges refers to as apathy, slowed speech, and flattened emotional responses. If you want to keep the nerve monster at bay, be sure to hit the hay.

Candidates do strange things when nervous during an interview. I interviewed an individual for a position and as we were about to get started, she felt compelled to share her thoughts about each of the interviewers' personality traits. It was very odd. I guess this was some sort of icebreaker that went astray. The interview team consisted of five people and she began the session by stating that she could determine our personalities and also determine what we were passionate about in life – all of this just by shaking our hands. And sure enough, she went around the room and told us. The actual interview wasn't much better. I would be surprised if she followed any of the suggestions that we outlined in this book. How did I know that she was nervous? She was fidgety throughout the interview, to the point in which it made members of the interview team uncomfortable. Plus, she told my assistant that she was extremely nervous as she was being escorted from the building following the interview. Remember, the interview isn't over until you are safely in your car driving home. Not having your nerves in check can cause you to do strange things.

CHAPTER 8

# What Hiring Managers are Looking For

CINDY CASTER IS an experienced manager and served in that role for twenty years at one of the largest property and casualty insurance companies in North America. She is also an attorney and has conducted over a hundred interviews and has personally been involved in the hiring of roughly 75 employees. Amazingly, all but one stayed with the company, for at least a minimum of five years. I asked Cindy to assist me with this part of the book because of her reputation for assembling high powered teams to perform the *stressful work of handling bodily injury insurance claims*.

 Handling insurance claims is not one of those jobs in which customers are calling to wish you a pleasant day. The only reasons why the public calls an auto insurance claims operation is because they've been involved in an accident, sued as a result of an accident or are demanding to be paid following an accident. Claims adjusters are a special breed. They are often called to provide court testimony, personally sued for alleged violations of state insurance laws and, to top it off, have the privilege of looking forward to a day filled with disgruntled customers who disagree with their every decision. Doing the job requires a thick skin and only a few are cut out for this type of work. Yet, Cindy has found a way to tap into the applicant talent pool and come out with high-potential employees who find success in this very tough industry. Cindy and I sat down to discuss what she looks for when interviewing job candidates.

First, Cindy shared the fact that she looks for people who are different from herself. She explained that it is important to develop a team of high energy people, but she does not want to have a group of clones. She looks for independent thinkers who can bring diversity of thought to the team, which makes for a more holistic and rich working environment.

When I asked Cindy what contributes to her success in selecting the right people, she addressed the importance of the interviewer doing the least amount of talking while encouraging the applicant to carry the conversation. As the applicant is talking, the interviewer should be listening. Listening for what? I asked. As Cindy puts it, she is listening to and focusing on everything about the candidate, including whether or not the actual question was answered; how the question was answered. She asks herself: Is the candidate demonstrating confidence; is the candidate demonstrating professionalism; is the candidate a good fit; how will customers take to his or her communication style and personality. Cindy points out that when hiring managers make poor hiring decisions, often it's because they were more focused on themselves opposed to listening to and learning from the candidate during the interview.

### SUCCESSFUL HIRING MANAGERS ARE TUNED IN TO ALL SIGNALS THAT THE CANDIDATE IS EMANATING AND THEY ARE DETERMINING IF THERE IS A CORRELATION BETWEEN WHAT IS SAID AND WHAT THE OTHER SENSES ARE EXPRESSING

Cindy says, "I simply let the candidate talk, and I don't talk." She goes on to say, "Do they have the qualities and, if they don't, can they learn them on the job?" When asked what she looks for in a candidate once the interview starts, Cindy has some very specific key observations:
- Are they honest? When the candidate is talking, Cindy is listening, looking and making a judgment about their honesty, sincerity,

## WHAT HIRING MANAGERS ARE LOOKING FOR

etc. She's looking into their eyes, facial expressions, and body language, all to see if they come across as trustworthy individuals. It's bothersome, Cindy points out, if they are looking at the ceiling when responding to a question or not focused on what's going on.
- Do they have strong communication skills? She is not only listening for the right answer, but also listening for how the response is articulated.
- What types of questions do the candidates ask: When it's time for the candidate to ask questions, it's a negative sign when they start off by asking how much vacation time they are allotted. "These questions in the first interview are clear indicators that they are less concerned about performing on the job than they are with the time spent away from the job." Cindy further states that she looks for people who convince her that they are interested in the job.
- Do they bad-mouth their prior employer? If they are willing to bad-mouth their prior employer, chances are they are willing to bad-mouth you. Plus, it's just poor judgment and is evidence of poor decision-making skills, a critical necessity in any service industry job.

We discussed "showstoppers" or things the candidate might do to guarantee them a zero chance of landing the job. First, showing up late to the interview pretty much ends your chances for consideration. "Flat tires, whatever, don't make a difference...," said Cindy. "It's that simple." Do whatever you have to do to arrive at the interview fifteen minutes before the interview starts. If you don't know where the interview is, travel there the day before to nail down your route. Check the weather reports for the day that you are scheduled to interview, and give yourself enough time to compensate for poor traffic and weather conditions. The bottom line is those who get there on time often get hired, and those who are late, don't. Another showstopper involves candidates who can't keep their emotions in check during the interview, (i.e., crying, inappropriate laughter, anger). Cindy shared with me the details of an interview that she conducted when suddenly the candidate started crying as she began to explain

◂ JUST GIVE ME THE DAMN JOB!

a situation that occurred at her last place of employment. On a personal level, the candidate may have had good reasons for becoming emotional, but there is never a good reason to do so during an interview. It's a showstopper when the candidate makes the interviewer feel uncomfortable. This may take the form of the candidate crying, sweating profusely, or demonstrating high levels of anxiety. Cindy explains that during the interview, she needs to feel a sense of trust and must believe that she would enjoy working with the candidate. Making the hiring manager feel uncomfortable or uneasy is not a way to foster that needed trust.

Cindy and I discussed those candidate attributes that impress her the most. She favored the candidates who researched the company prior to the interview: "How much do they know about us? By researching the company, the candidate is showing me a little of their work ethic and preparation skills." As for advice that she would give any candidate, Cindy says they should focus on the following:

- Be yourself – Check that… "Be your <u>BEST</u> self"
- Don't try to over-impress
- Be authentic

Much of what we discussed in this chapter, we touched on throughout the book. If you are not seeing a pattern, you should. When you establish a theme for the interview and sufficiently prepare, your responses will be in sync with all of your body's senses. By now, you should understand that while the interviewer is listening to what you say, he or she is also making a determination whether what you say is in lockstep with your overall presentation and demeanor. Make sure that everything about you is emanating the same powerful message. Be confident. You are prepared, so there is no reason to be anything other than confident. That feeling of confidence comes with preparation and will be your best friend during the interview. Be positive and lastly, be knowledgeable. The key to impressing the Cindy Casters of the world during an interview is preparation, preparation, preparation! Got it? Okay, let's move on.

CHAPTER 9

# Dress Code for the Interview

AH YES, WHAT to wear? It's the most basic question for each and every one of us who gets up in the morning and prepares for that journey to the office. Although all of our "offices" may be unique, what we wear still requires considerable thought. Our wardrobe says a lot about who we are as an individual. It forms a pretty strong impression in the minds of the people with whom we work and interact and with whom we interview.

> **BEFORE OTHERS FORM AN IMPRESSION ABOUT YOU BASED ON YOUR WORDS, THEY ARE FORMING AN IMPRESSION BASED ON YOUR ATTIRE.**

Let's talk about dressing for the interview. And first, I'll state for the record that I am no expert in this area. However, I will also state that the candidate who brings the complete package to the interview, (i.e., being prepared, confident, and looking the part) is the one that I'm going to remember most during deliberations following the interview.

The job for which you are interviewing will have a great deal to do with how you dress for the position. If, for example, you are applying for a job at The Gap clothing store, Limited, or The Express, it may be appropriate to dress for the interview in a manner that reflects the clothing that you will sell. In this case, the employee is somewhat of a walking advertisement for the store. Therefore, to wear high-end jeans accompanied by the latest design of sneakers may be perfectly okay. Regardless of the company, the rule of thumb is to look professional, and as Cindy pointed out in the last chapter, "be your Best self." Let's say that you are interviewing for a factory job and the working conditions often leave the employees looking a bit frayed by the end of the day. This does not mean that you want to dress for the interview looking the same way as the factory workers currently on the floor. But, you should wear clothes that were just cleaned and pressed and that present you in the best possible light. It doesn't matter if you are the best looking and best dressed person who interviewed for the factory job that day. However, the manager interviewing you will notice the extra effort that you went through to prepare for the interview and it can only help your chances of landing the job.

In the mid 1980's, a trend started to overtake North American companies in which it was no longer mandatory to wear professional business attire to the office. This cultural shift occurred not because senior management had a burning desire to change the landscape of the corporate wardrobe scene. The initial change from business wear to business-casual resulted from the need to attract information technologists and computer scientists to their companies. The competition was fierce for these skill sets in the 1980s and 1990s. In fact, it became so competitive during this period that companies were actually including perks such as cars to attract the top computer science graduates. Besides the cars, one of the more common perks demanded by these up-and-coming stars was the opportunity to dress casually at work. Now, many organizations have held on to the business-casual model that became all the rage just twenty years earlier. Although business casual dress is now appropriate in many office settings, it is not necessarily appropriate for the interview. When in doubt, wear professional business attire to the interview. There are numerous websites out there that will give you the dos and don'ts of dressing for the interview. However, I want to share a few here, as well, under the guise of *keeping it real*.

## DRESS CODE FOR THE INTERVIEW

1. Easy on the perfume and cologne – As a hiring manager, I don't want to be overcome by the smell of cologne or perfume. You want to control the focus during the interview on your abilities to perform on the job. You don't want to add any distractions which derail your theme.
2. Short skirts, low cut tops don't work – I know in the movies that the sexy-dressed lady always gets the position. If a man hires you, as a woman, for such reasons, he is obviously looking for something more than talent. In reality, it will only extend your time on the unemployment line. Be it male or female, dress professionally.
3. Keep the brown suit at home – I don't know why, but when I think of men in brown suits, I can't help but think of Willy in Arthur Miller's 1949 classic play, Death of a Salesman.[6] Brown suits during an interview seem to represent the poster child for low self-esteem. Stay with the blues, grays and blacks. Pinstripes in either of these colors are fine.
4. Too much jewelry is not a good thing – A nice touch of jewelry worn during the interview can add class and professional elegance to your overall appearance. Too much jewelry can make you appear superficial and untrustworthy.

How you dress for the interview is a part of your overall theme. Your attire will complement all of the other measures that you have taken to land the job. This is a day that you must be at your very best. If this requires your going out and purchasing a new outfit, then do it. Take care to ensure that your outfit selection is in lockstep with who you are and how you want to be perceived. You want to nail down this job now. This is the time to pull out all of the stops and go for it.

---

[6] Bloom, Harold, ed. *Arthur Miller's "Death of a Salesman."* New York: Chelsea House, 1988

CHAPTER **10**

# Nail these Questions and You Nail the Job

COMPANIES HAVE A lot at stake when they bring a new employee into their organization. Nothing is worse, from a hiring manager's perspective, than selecting the wrong candidate. They want to get it right on the first try. The interview is a major part of the process to determine if you are the right fit for the job. Other parts of the selection process include background checks and checking references. But, you don't even get to the background and reference checks if you don't pass the interview portion. Interview questions are designed to determine (1) if you are who you say you are, (2) if you have the skills needed for the job for which you are interviewing, (3) if you are reliable, and (4) if you have the potential to advance within the company. Hiring managers interview job applicants from the premise that the best indicator of future performance is past performance. So, expect numerous questions about your past behavior.

What we will do for the remainder of this chapter is identify the most common questions that you can expect during the interview and discuss what you should take into consideration as part of your response. If you are adequately prepared to answer the following interview questions, you will also be more than prepared to address the unexpected questions as well. So let's get to work.

## 1. Please discuss the skills and background that you believe best qualify you for the position for which you are applying?

You can bet the ranch on it – you are going to get this question. The interviewer is asking you - *why are you here?* To best respond to this question, you will need to refer to the two preparation resources that we discussed earlier – the company's website and the job advertisement to which you responded, that earned you the interview.

During your preparation, spend time matching the core competencies of the job with your own set of skills. Write them down and repeat them back until you can recite them in your sleep. When you get to the interview and the question is raised, specifically answer the question by referring to your skills, which you matched up to the job requirements during your preparation. Keep your responses in a conversational tone. This is the part of the interview in which you want to discuss your previous training, education, and experience. In your response, briefly discuss how you applied your training, education, and experience in your last position. By studying the company's website, you will gain context for how to structure your response. Review the company's mission statement and value statement. Review the history of the company. This information will help you identify with the company and with the interviewers during the interview.

## 2. Why are you leaving your current job?

The interviewer wants to know whether you were fired, are you about to be fired, or are you leaving on bad terms. Being fired from a job is not a showstopper from getting hired on the next job. But you have some explaining to do. The interviewer is simply looking to better understand the circumstances of your previous and current situation. If you were terminated, laid off, downsized or whatever they are calling it these days, your response must be well-thought-out. You don't want to get caught stumbling and mumbling through this question. In today's environment, being laid off is quite common and understandable from the interviewer's perspective. It is a little easier to answer the question if you are interviewing while still with the company that you are planning to leave. Your reasons might include that you are looking to better yourself, looking for a more stable environment, looking to work in a particular field, looking to be challenged. The key to these questions is to ground your response on business reasons opposed to personal ones. For example, you want to downplay reasons such as, I want to live in this particular area; I want to get back closer to family; I want to live in a warm-weather climate. The interviewer could care less about your desire to retire in that location or about you wanting to live in a warmer climate. All of your responses should connect you and your skills to the job. If you were laid off, that may be the simplest response – *I was laid off*. But, be sure to follow up your response with what you can bring to the position if hired. And under no circumstance should you bad-mouth your previous employer. Sure, there may be certain conditions that you weren't fond of in your last job, but it won't help you in the long run to spend time and negative energy on a previous negative experience. If you were terminated from your last job, the circumstances of that termination will determine how you handle this question. Lying is never a good idea. If you were let go, then say so. But follow up with what you have learned from the experience and how that growth will make you a better employee for this current opportunity. Keep it positive and keep it brief. Again, this is not the time to bad-mouth your former employer. The hiring manager is interested in your entire package. There are strengths and weaknesses with every candidate and you want to accentuate the strengths while deemphasizing the weaknesses.

## 3. During your last job, describe a situation where you had to complete a task within a specific timeframe that you considered unreasonable. What did you do to address the dilemma?

This is a situational question, which comes in many forms. The purpose of situational questions is to better understand how you handle diversity on the job. Are you combative in stressful situations? How do you get along with people? Are you capable of coming up with original solutions to solve problems? Or, are you one to simply go with the flow? Situational questions also provide the interviewer with some idea of how you think on your feet. They are aware, as you are responding, if you had to hesitate for an extended period of time before you answered. Were you squirming through your response because you hadn't given the question enough thought? Or were you quick on your feet, providing an answer that underscored your overall interview preparation? It is impossible to predict all of the situational questions that you might be asked. But if you anticipate and prepare for a few, you will be ready to answer the unexpected ones as well. During your prep, list four or five situational questions that are a possibility based on your previous work experience and the job for which you're applying. It doesn't make a difference if you aren't asked the specific questions for which you've prepared. The act of going through the exercise will assist you immensely in answering any of the situational questions asked. Other situational questions may be formed as follows:

- Share with us a time when you didn't get along with a co-worker. How did you handle the conflict?
- Discuss a situation when your supervisor gave you an assignment with which you didn't agree. How did you handle your disagreement with the boss?
- Describe a time, while working for your last employer, in which you exceeded in performing a specific job expectation. What was it and what do you attribute to your success?
- Describe a time when you were unsuccessful in completing a specific job assignment. What do you attribute to your lack of success?

If you are caught by surprise by a specific question and just can't think of a response, ask the interviewer if you can come back to it. Ten times out of ten, the interviewer will accommodate. But, be sure

## NAIL THESE QUESTIONS AND YOU NAIL THE JOB

that you do eventually answer the question. If the situation in the question has never come up in your experience, then say so. But you can also answer the question by explaining that *if such a situation did occur, I would handle it like...* and then explain how you would address the situation.

### 4. If I were to ask your former supervisor and co-workers about your work performance, what would they say about you?

This is not a trick question. But it is clever in the sense that the question isn't asking you to discuss your own work performance. Instead, the question is asking you to discuss what others would say about you regarding your work performance. Interviewers know that they are more likely to get the most genuine response if the question is posed in the above referenced manner. Don't fall for the clever sleight of hand. You need to answer this question as if they are asking you to speak about you. Address your strengths and always phrase the response in a way that feeds into the needs and expectations of the job for which you are applying. Don't stray from your theme.

### 5. What are your strengths and what are your weaknesses?

The interviewer wants to know what you are good at and where do you have problems. Earlier in the book, we discussed how to address questions regarding your weaknesses during the interview. As a recap, you want to minimize your weaknesses by embracing them as part of your strengths. Keep in mind that this is not a therapy session - it's an interview. This is not the time or place to reveal all of your innermost secrets. Be sure to spend considerable time talking about your strengths. You must prepare for this question. As you tout your strengths, it is also important to support your self-promotion with evidence of your strengths in action. Everyone will come into the interview ready to run off a list of strengths that they believe are germane to the job. But few will come to the interview ready to support their discussion with actual examples in which they have used their strengths to achieve an organizational objective. That is…everyone except you!

## 6. Describe your ideal boss.

This question is another way for the interviewer to get to know you. What makes you tick? How do you really interact with peers and with supervisors? The interviewer wants to know more about your personality. He or she wants to know how you will handle conflict with your boss. Is there a match between you, the interviewee, and your potential boss, who probably is the one asking the question? In responding to this question, it is important to communicate that you respect candor in a supervisor. How you get that point across is up to you. But you do want to project that you are someone who can handle critical feedback as well as learn from it. You want to take this opportunity to impress upon the interviewer your ability to work independently, if independence is germane to the position. You want to let the interviewer know that you favor a work environment where you are trusted to make decisions and be held accountable for those decisions. Wanting to make decisions is one thing, but such a response is incomplete unless you add that you want to be held accountable for those decisions as well. These types of responses will send a message to the interviewer that you are reliable and that you are someone who is willing to take on responsibility and be held accountable for the required outcome.

## 7. How did you prepare for today's interview?

How you prepared for the interview speaks volumes about how you will prepare for assignments on the job. You have nothing to be ashamed of in answering this question truthfully. Speak to the fact that you studied their company's website. If you contacted the company and spoke to customer sales reps, factory workers, etc. to learn more about the job, tell them so. When I interviewed for a regional superintendent position for a major insurance carrier, I spoke with a few company sales agents beforehand to learn what they considered to be the most challenging customer service issues with reference to the company. You better believe that this went a long way when I answered the "how did I prepare" question. If I wasn't a serious candidate before, I surely was after I answered that question. I was viewed as someone willing to go the extra mile. The interviewer will view you the same way if you can demonstrate that you went the extra mile in preparing for the interview.

## 8. In reviewing your resume, I see a six month gap in your employment, please explain.

Do not the fumble the ball here. If you have major gaps between jobs on your resume, the interviewer is going to ask you about them. It is not a crime to be out of work. If you were out of work and spent that time looking for a job, say so during the interview. Other reasons for employment gaps may include going back to school, a family member going back to school, taking care of a sick relative and the list goes on. The key here is honesty. You will be asked the question.

## 9. Should we hire you for the position, what are your short and long term professional goals?

Should you join their ranks, interviewers genuinely want to know your aspirations. If you are the right candidate, this question and your reply, could be the start of helping you achieve your long term goals. If you are asked this question, you are expected to have some goals and personal aspirations, both short and long term. However, you do not want to over shoot. In other words, stating that you plan to have the hiring manager's job in the next twelve months might be a stretch and can come across as an overly aggressive employee. Your research will help you determine how far you want to stretch on this question. For most entry level positions, you want to focus short term goals on learning the job and gaining the confidence of those who entrusted you with the position. Your longer term goals may address such things as taking on more responsibility, including a management position. But, if a position in management is not what you're striving for, that's okay too. When I interviewed for my first job out of college and was asked this question, I responded to the interviewer by letting them know that I wanted to continue to improve in my craft, learn more about other opportunities within the company, and be prepared for those opportunities when they came my way. However, your response will depend greatly on the job itself.

## 10. On a scale of 1 to 10 (1 being the weakest and 10 being the strongest), indicate how you would describe yourself in the following areas:

| # | Description | Skill Set Ranking Scale 1 through 10 1 = Weakest / 10 = Strongest |
|---|---|---|
|  | Oral Presentation Skills |  |
|  | Written Communication |  |
|  | Technological Skills |  |
|  | Organizational Skills |  |
|  | Critical Thinking Skills |  |

During the interview, it would not be uncommon for the interviewer to ask you to rank a group of skill sets as they apply to your self-perception. The above list is a simple example, but the skill sets can range from 5, 10 or more areas to rank. Once you rank the skill sets, the follow up question will always be, why did you rank skill set #2 so low or why did you rank skill set #5 so high. This exercise, which is playing out during the interview, helps the interviewer (1)

## NAIL THESE QUESTIONS AND YOU NAIL THE JOB

better understand how you perceive your strengths and weaknesses, (2) gain additional insight into your overall persona, (3) determine if there is alignment between your interview presentation thus far and how you responded to each skill set self-critique, and (4) assess your confidence level in the areas that matter. In responding to any sort of self-assessment question, it is important to be truthful and honest with yourself. If you have strong oral presentation skills, don't be bashful in ranking yourself a 10! If you are not as strong in your writing skills, you will want to rank yourself accordingly. Here are a couple of hints to answering these self-assessment questions:

Although their scale is 1 through 10. You don't have to respond using the same measures. If you are very weak in an area, their "5" can be your "7."

Interviewers will usually be critical about low scores in the area of organizational skills. And when a self-assessment ranking is part of the interview, I guarantee you that one of the assessments will be on organization. Poor organization affects every facet of the job, any job. The good news in improving organizational skills comes down to areas that are all under your control - attitude, commitment, and time management. So, be sure to put yourself in a position where you can score high in this area.

A score of perfect 10s is great during Olympic competition, but it will lead to suspicion on a self-assessment exercise. As far as I know, there was only one perfect man in human history. Unless you are Him, give yourself some room to improve.

## 11. How would you handle a situation in which you made a recommendation to your boss that she rejected and decided to go in a completely different direction?

In addition to wanting to know if you can perform on the job, the employer also wants to know what your hot buttons are. Are you willing to adapt to change? This type of situational question helps the employer understand how you will handle conflict. Bottom line, are you a cancer or are you the cure? And you definitely want to be the cure. Being the cure does not mean that you are willing to roll over and simply succumb to anything and everything. No one wants a person who can't think for himself or herself. But, at the end of the day, are you willing to support the decisions of the team?

## 12. What is it about this job that appeals to you most?

The purpose of this question is to help reveal how well you prepared for the interview and how much you know about the company. You can't answer this question unless you know something about the company and the position for which you are applying. The interviewer is also gauging your level of interest in the job. An applicant should be excited when answering this particular question. This is the reason why you are here and it is why you went through all of the preparation work. For some jobs, the opportunity to work and earn a living may be the primary draw of the position; and it is okay if this is the draw for you. But the excitement and energy that you reveal in expressing the appeal of the position is crucial in responding to this question. I recall when I was interviewing for a teaching position at the University of Cincinnati. I was in my mid 20s at the time, and the opportunity to fulfill my dream job was close to becoming a reality. Yes, I was very excited. My energy was at an all time high. During the interview, I was asked what it was about this opportunity that appealed to me. My eyes must have told the story before I even started answering the question. I discussed how much it meant to me to have a role in someone else's success. I talked about having the opportunity to be affiliated with such an outstanding university. I discussed my responsibility to the academic community and to the business community in preparing the leaders of tomorrow. My excitement was contagious -- it was shared throughout the room. When you have the opportunity to discuss what appeals to you about the job, take the opportunity to express your feelings not only in words but also through your overall energy level.

## 13. Have you applied for any other positions besides this one?

Call it inquisitive, curious, or prying, it is a common question when the skill sets that you are bringing to the table are in high demand. Interviewers want to know what companies they are competing against. Regardless of whether this is your only interview or your fifth, keep a little pressure on this group by advising them that there are a few other companies in the running. Always remember that interviewing is a two-way street. They are not only interviewing you, but you are interviewing them as well.

## 14. What is your biggest regret as it relates to your last job?

With many of these questions, the interviewer is attempting to peel the meat off of the bones, and get down to the bare essence of who you really are. It's gone beyond the *tell-me-about-yourself* type of question. Now, the questions are requiring you to be very specific in your response. You can't wing it. You must think about it and your response must be genuine. I'm just a tad leery of applicants who have no regrets or wouldn't have changed a thing in their last position. It doesn't necessarily mean that such a response is a show stopper, but it does raise my spider-senses (you old Spider Man fans will understand what I'm talking about). Personally, I don't recall a job in which I wouldn't have done something different if I had it to do all over again. If you don't have any regrets, I am not suggesting that you make one up. What is important is that you are prepared for the question and that you remember that this is not a counseling session with your therapist. Always think about threading a positive outcome in your response.

## 15. What would you consider to be your most gratifying experience on your last job?

Unlike the last question, you must have an example or examples about your most gratifying experiences in your last job. And, these experiences must be positive. *"My most gratifying experience at my last job is when I walked out of the building for the last time and told my boss to take this job and shove it,"* is not an example of a positive response. Regardless of how difficult your last assignment was, it is never a good idea to talk negatively about your prior employer during an interview.

## 16. Based on what you know about the position that you are applying for, what areas concern you the most?

Think about it this way – the company that is seriously thinking about hiring you will invest a considerable amount of time, money and effort should they bring you on board. Hiring a new employee is one of the most substantial costs that a company will incur, second only to the cost of the building itself. So it should not surprise you that they are going to ask questions that will help them to better understand everything about you, including what concerns you the most about the job. They don't want a potential situation where you are hired and, once in the role, they find out that you are overwhelmed by some anxiety that they had no way of knowing about beforehand. Are you concerned about workload, are you concerned about speaking to large groups, are you concerned about learning a new computer system, or are you concerned about the work hours? Whatever you may be concerned about, the company wants to know in order to help you overcome the issue or assess whether this is the right job for you. In answering this question, you want to stay away from matters which may reflect on your apprehension of whether you can perform. And this is not one of those questions about which you must have a concern. If you don't have any concerns, say so and simply let them know that you are ready to get started. As we have discussed numerous times on previous occasions, any answer you give to any question must be positive and this question is no different.

## 17. Given that this is a salaried position, how many hours per week do you anticipate working?

Many jobs classified as professional jobs are salaried positions. Often, these jobs were and still are referred to as white-collar jobs. However, we won't use the term *white-collar* here as it relates to the job market. I find the term sexist and a throwback to a time when only men held white-collar positions, hence the name white-collar jobs. Many women now serve in professional positions and fall under the salary pay scale. Salaried positions, also referred to as exempt status classification, simply mean that employee pay is not based on hourly time worked during the day or week. This is compared to non-exempt positions in which employees' pay is based on time worked during the day or week. When you are asked the question in an interview, the employer wants to get a fix on your work habits. For example, let's say that the employer understands that, to be effective in the position, it will take at least 50 hours per week to do the job. If the applicant responds to the question by stating that he or she plans to work about 40 hours per week, such a response could raise questions pertaining to your overall work ethic. Not knowing the specifics of the job, responding to this question in terms of hours may be difficult. But you should let the employer know that you will work as long as it takes to get the job done. And, if you are comfortable speaking in terms of number of hours, 45 to 55 hours per week sounds better than 35 to 45 hours per week. Interestingly enough, stating too high a number can raise additional questions about your time management skills. If, for example, you respond to this question by stating that you plan to put 75 hours a week into the job, do not be surprised with the follow up question, "Why do you believe that it will take you this amount of time to get the job done?"

In addition to the previous set of questions, the next set of questions is routinely asked of applicants interviewing for management positions. What's quite interesting about management interviews is that the majority of the questions (about 85%) will address your human interaction characteristics and skills while the remaining questions will focus on whether you can do the technical aspects of the job. There is already an assumption that you can do the technical part – if there wasn't you would not have gotten this far in the interview process. Given that the majority of managerial functions are about relationships and human interaction, don't be surprised that the majority of the questions will address your ability to interact with people.

## 18. What is your management style?

You are going to be asked this question. In fact, I have never interviewed for a management position in which I did not get this question and, often, I got the question more than once during the same interview. Describing your management style is the most important question that will be asked from the interviewer's perspective. Now, for all of you college graduates with a degree in some business-related field, please leave your textbook theories about different management styles at home when addressing this question. No one is interested in hearing you spout off whether you are a Theory X or Theory Y manager. What the interviewer wants to know is if you have what it takes to effectively lead people in a way that aligns with the company's culture or will your style contribute to an employee revolt? Therefore, explain what you intend to do and how you plan to get it done. Allow me to relate an amusing story. When I graduated from college, I was asked to explain my management style for a position for which I was applying. I went into my Theory X approach and I talked about situational and transformational leadership. And all the time that I am speaking, my soon-to-be boss is nodding his head. Following my answer, he went on to the next question. Therefore, I assumed that I was hitting the mark. Well, about six months after I was hired, my boss and I met for a beer after work. It was then that he told me that he didn't have a clue what the heck I was talking about when I responded to the question of management style. However, I guess I did impress him, in spite of myself, in other areas. Wow, did I ever learn my lesson from that screw up.

Your management style is whatever it is. If you act one way, don't state for the sake of the interview that you act a different way. You are who you are and if you present something different, you are going to be exposed as soon as you get into the role. Today, I answer the management style question quite differently than I did 26 years ago. I extend a great deal of effort in hiring the best people that I can find. I make sure that they are trained and then I basically get out of their way and expect them to perform as advertised. I am a candid manager. If the employee is not performing to my expectations, they will be the first to know and they will also understand the inevitable outcome if their performance does not improve. I like surrounding myself with people a lot smarter than me because I will delegate meaningful responsibilities to them. With responsibility comes accountability, meaning that I hold employees accountable for the results that fall under their purview. I prefer, and deliberately work to create, a working atmosphere in which employees have fun and feel good about coming to work. After doing this sort of thing for as long as I have, I've concluded that most people respect and appreciate it if you are candid with them. This is how I approach management and it seems to work for me. As you answer this question, keep it basic and tell them how you plan to approach things. My management style is not perfect. I have not always gotten it right. And it is perfectly acceptable if your approach is totally different from mine. I have worked with colleagues who have been quite successful using a very authoritative management approach. They make all of the meaningful decisions and their employees' only responsibility is to carry out their directives. Again, remember what the interviewer is interested in – does your management style align with the company's organizational culture and will your style serve to create a unified operation or cause an employee revolt?

## 19. If hired, how will you spend your first week on the job?

Sometimes this question will have you outlining your first six months on the job. What thought have you given to the role, where do you plan to lead this unit or department, and how do you plan to get there? Don't get nervous. The interviewer does not expect you to lay out for them a strategic plan with charts and graphs. They want to know, in general terms, your thoughts for moving the operation forward. In some cases, providing such information is part of the request in the initial application package. It is great when you have the opportunity to share your thoughts about leading the operation as part of your application package. Doing so offers you with another preparation tool to which you can refer during the interview. However, in most cases, you will be expected to address the question during the interview. To best prepare for this question, you will need to review your preparation resources, i.e. job advertisement, company website, and industry data. Frame in your own mind how the company is positioned in the industry; understand the organizational structure and their basic workflow processes. You may not be able to acquire all of this information, but ascertain as much as you can. There is a chance that not all of this information will be needed to respond to the question. Regardless, the information will help you to articulate a well crafted response. And, the longer the timeframe, three months or six months, the better prepared you will be if you do the research.

As you start any new job, the first thing that you should do is to get to know the people that are working for you. Meet with them one-on-one. Find out what their concerns are. During the first few days, you should be in the information gathering stage. However, you should be ready to handle situations that need to be addressed as soon as possible. In some situations, taking time to gather information may be a luxury that you don't have. Personnel changes may be needed and the top brass is waiting on you to get on board to make the changes. If personnel changes are needed, you want to make the changes sooner rather than later. But, be willing to first understand the landscape and learn what hot fixes require your immediate attention. After answering the question, I would pose the question back to the interviewer of what areas do they see needing immediate attention.

When answering this question, start strong with getting to know your people, but be ready to transition from knowing your people to ACTION! Think in terms of becoming quickly familiar with the operation so you can position yourself to make recommendations for better serving your stakeholders. Think in terms of action once you move off of the "knowing your people" line. The reason why there is an opening in the position that for which you're interviewing may be because the last person in the job did not address matters urgently enough. During the interview, you want to communicate your desire to quickly get up to speed, address any immediate needs and/or concerns that have been shelved in anticipation of your arrival and move the unit along in the direction that meets the objectives set by senior leadership.

## 20. If I were to ask your former and most challenging employee about your management style, what would they say about you?

Yes, we are back to that management style question again. But, this question has a little different twist. You've already answered what you believe your management style to be. Now, the interviewer is asking if your most challenging employee agrees with your own self-assessment. If this is your first management position, then this question will not apply to you. But, if you have been in other management positions, you will be able to relate. Challenging employees take up considerable time to manage and neither you nor the employee is happy about it. The interviewer is not expecting a happy-ending type of response from you. They simply want to gauge your leadership tenacity under difficult circumstances. Chances are if you are asked this question, there is a challenging employee waiting for you when you get the job. I have had challenging employees who didn't like me when I confronted them about their work performance and they probably don't like me now. And, I have worked with others whom I was able to redirect onto a positive path. But, regardless of the employee, my approach was the same – I was candid with them in terms of where they needed to improve, gave them an opportunity to improve, and if they did not improve, I dismissed them. It is okay for you to respond to this question with the acknowledgement that your challenging employee did not appreciate your management style if such was the case. As long as you demonstrate consistency in your approach and fairness, you will do fine.

## 21. Describe for us a situation in your prior management experience where you had to counsel a poorly performing employee? What was the situation and what was the outcome?

Top performers are easy to manage. In fact, such performance evaluations are often fun. When the grade is an "A," why shouldn't it be? Where the rubber meets the road for assessing a manager's leadership courage, potential employers observe how they might manage poor performers. The interviewer wants to know if you are fair and whether you have the leadership courage to make the difficult decisions as it relates to firing or demoting a poor performer. The interviewer is not asking you to reveal personnel and/or private information. But you should respond with the understanding that the interviewer is looking for someone who has a combination of fairness and the leadership courage to make the difficult decisions.

CHAPTER **11**

# Conclusion

## Finding a job when you have a criminal record

I HAVE DEVOTED this book to how to nail a job once you secure the interview. But I also want to refer briefly to a forgotten group – people looking for work who have a criminal record. As part of my service to the community, I have had the privilege of working with adults who have recently been released from prison for non-violent offenses and are looking for employment.

There is nothing more difficult than finding legitimate employment for people who have a criminal record. It is difficult enough to find a job when you don't have a criminal background. But once you are tagged as an ex-offender, it can be nearly impossible in both healthy and unhealthy economies. Most companies simply aren't willing to take a chance. From the company's perspective, why should they run the risk of hiring an ex-offender when there is an overabundance of job applicants who don't carry that baggage? Although it is difficult, it is not impossible to find gainful employment with a criminal record. But it requires incredible work, extra effort, preparation, commitment and patience.

There are companies and organizations that are willing to hire ex-offenders. Many church groups offer re-entry training programs and work with companies who are committed to hiring ex-offenders who have gone through such programs. Your church is a great place to start if you or anyone you know is in need of such services. If your church does not have a re-entry training program, they will be able to guide you to where such programs exist.

As I meet with such individuals, I encourage them to take advantage of volunteer opportunities. By volunteering your time and energies to a cause, you are accomplishing two very important requirements for gaining re-entry into the job market. First, you are rebuilding a positive track record. The last experience you list on your resume does not have to be the work that you performed while incarcerated. Volunteer work is legitimate work and is very appropriate to list as experience. Secondly, volunteering grants others the opportunity to form their perceptions of you and opinions about you based on what they see and not totally on what they have read or have been told. It is not uncommon for ex-offenders to start or restart their working career as volunteers and end up employed at the same company.

With a criminal record, you have to convince potential employers that you have turned the corner and are well on the path to a legitimate, productive, and a meaningful life. One way to help convince such employers is to return to school and complete your education. If you don't have a high school degree, you MUST go back and complete your GED or high school diploma. There are countless trade schools that one can attend to gain initial skills or enhance skills in a particular area of interest. Community colleges have open enrollment programs whereby it is not required for the student applicant to fulfill a minimum entry examination score to take courses. Regardless of the educational path sought, it sends a strong message to potential employers when you can show that you have completed a training program or an educational program of some sort. Lastly, don't dismiss the opportunity to go into business for yourself. One gentleman with whom I worked had a criminal background. He purchased a pair of hair clippers and started cutting

## CONCLUSION

hair for clients in his own home. His business eventually became too large for his home, necessitating the rental of a small office space to handle his business growth. It is not my intent to sugarcoat how difficult it is to find employment if you have a criminal record. Nor do I want to leave you with the impression that finding such employment is impossible. But it requires major league work and commitment on your part.

The number one question I get from people with a criminal record is, *If I do get the interview, should I tell them about my incarceration?* The answer is yes. You must tell them. If you don't, they are going to find out and fire you for being dishonest. Most companies, even the small ones, are requiring background checks on new hires. For companies that don't do background checks, they can easily check you out simply by running your name through the Internet. I cannot say that you won't get fired anyway. But personally I would have more respect for an individual who told me about their incarceration up front rather than learning about it on my own. Inform your potential employer about your incarceration sooner rather than later. It is important to establish the potential employer/employee relationship with eyes wide open from everyone's perspective. When you control the conversation upfront about your incarceration, it becomes a burden that you no longer have to tackle when the potential employer is ready to reach out and take a chance on you.

## Negotiating your starting pay

Negotiating a starting salary can be a tricky song and dance. You don't want to dampen the positive feelings that the hiring manager has for you through the process of countering their starting pay offer with a counter offer of your own. Nor do you want to waste everyone's time if their starting offer is too low for you to accept. There is also the question of when to discuss pay. Do you bring it up during the interview? And, if so, at what point do you discuss starting

### JUST GIVE ME THE DAMN JOB!

pay? Job applicants tend to think differently about this subject than do hiring managers. Job applicants are fearful to breech the subject while hiring managers expect the topic to come up. Of course, it all depends on the type and level of the job. It is more likely to negotiate starting salaries in management and/or special skill positions than it is for jobs in which the skills are plentiful in the marketplace. But it is not off limits to negotiate your starting pay even in jobs where the skills are plentiful. Understand that starting compensation involves more than pay. Compensation also involves benefits including medical insurance and Permission Time Off (PTO). Some companies are willing to increase the pay in lieu of some other benefit. For example, if you live in a household in which the spouse also works and has an insurance plan that covers you both, you may want to negotiate with your potential employer an increase in starting pay instead of the insurance plan that you don't need. As expensive as insurance plans are at present, many companies will go for such an option.

The best negotiator is the job applicant who is willing to walk away from the job opportunity if the company can't meet his or her demands. It is sort of like negotiating for a new car. You don't have any negotiating power if that new shiny red car must go home with you, come what may. The salesperson knows that he or she can sell you that car for the list price and, therefore, doesn't have to negotiate. Negotiating your starting pay is no different. A close friend shared with me a story in which he walked away from a job offer when he realized that the offer was not going to be enough for him to maintain the lifestyle to which he was accustomed. He put the numbers to pen and pad and came up with a figure that he felt was necessary for him to take the job. He countered the company's offer. They would not budge, and he walked away from the opportunity. Although my friend did not end up working for the company, he was negotiating from a position of strength because he was willing to walk away. If you are not willing to walk away, tread lightly in this dance.

Earlier in the book, we talked about having a few questions

## CONCLUSION

ready for the interviewer. In chapter 8, Cindy Caster noted that when she interviews candidates, she is interested in the types of questions that they ask to determine if they are interested in the job or just interested in the money. That's what makes this topic so difficult. You must have a discussion about pay, but you don't want to come across as if pay is the only thing in which you're interested. As a rule of thumb, you should not broach the subject of pay on the first interview. The first interview is more for the company to learn who you are and to determine if they want to invite you back for a more extensive screening. Secondly, if the interviewer doesn't initiate the discussion about starting pay, you can easily find out what the pay is by searching the website, salaries.com on the Internet. Once you get a better feeling about the company and it appears that they are interested in you, it is perfectly okay to bring up the salary. But you still may have to go through the song and dance routine. Let's say you're in the second interview. Nothing about starting pay has been discussed yet. It looks like you are the person for the job and you ask, "The job appears to be just want I'm looking for, but I would like to know how much the starting salary is." The response is something like, "Good question. The starting salary is forty-five thousand per year. Is that what you had in mind?" No job offer has been extended yet. So do you want to negotiate a salary where, in fact, no offer has been made? You can respond with an "It's in the ballpark and I am still very interested in the job" line. Or you can respond with, "Is this a job offer?" My point is, it is now a two-step dance that you have entered into. I actually prefer to enter into salary negotiations after the job has been offered. I find that you, the job applicant, are in a stronger position to get them to move once they have committed to you through the job offer.

## Aptitude and personality testing

Many employers now require candidates seeking certain professional jobs to go through some form of profile testing. Aptitude tests are administered to candidates for jobs that require high levels of cognition skills, i.e., thinking, reasoning and remembering. Personality tests are usually required for positions with high levels of consumer interaction such as commission sales and customer service positions. Profile testing is often used because employers believe that the interview itself is not enough to determine if the candidate can perform the job. A good friend of mine applied for a sales position at a major company, but was rejected after he did not score in the acceptable range on the personality test. He was disappointed to the extent of demanding a full explanation of how the score was calculated. He contacted me to further vent over not being granted the job opportunity when he thought that his initial screening interview went quite well. I explained to him that he can't look at these profile tests in the sense of a pass or fail grade. Nor should they be viewed as an indictment of you, the person. Personal profile tests are structured to measure the candidate's potential for success in a specific job based on how he or she perceives other social, professional, technical and personal situations that can be compared to the activities associated with the job. If you, the applicant, scores in the lower percentile compared to other applicants, it is unlikely that the employer is going to proceed any further with you in the hiring process. However, such scores don't mean that you will be unsuccessful in the particular field that you applied for or aspire to work in. However, taking such tests does present an opportunity to further identify where your strengths and weaknesses are so you can focus your energies on areas in which you are most likely to be successful. In fact, you don't have to wait for the interview to take an aptitude or a personality profile test. You can find them online and should take these tests as part of the *knowing thyself* stage of your interview preparation. By doing so, you can target those opportunities that best reflect your strengths.

I am not a big proponent of profiling type tests for the purpose of making hiring decisions. In fact, I have had numerous exchanges with Human Resource types regarding their usefulness. I have found that these tests often don't take into consideration cultural differences that we all share and they tend to place little weight on the passion, drive and commitment that one is willing to bring to the position. I can't imagine where I would be if I allowed some third party testing service to dictate my future. But understand that more and more organizations are using such testing mechanisms as a screening tool to weed out potential candidates. Do not view these tests as an indictment on you. But do accept their outcomes as an opportunity to help carve out your niche or as the fuel needed to ignite your passion toward pursuing the position or career of your dreams.

## Thank you letters

After all of the interviews are done, should you write a thank-you letter? The answer is yes. As a society, it seems that we have gotten away from writing thank-you letters following an interview and I'm not sure why. I think, in part, it may be due to the change in our society as it relates to the expectations we have of one another. We have become a culture that demands everything to be faster and we have bought into the notion that speed alone translates into better human relations absent everything else we've learned concerning how to treat people and how we expect to be treated. Case in point – when did it become okay to send and receive a holiday greeting card through the Internet? How much thought goes into going online, pulling up a greeting card from some website and sending it to a friend or loved one? The answer is none. Yet, this is what we have been reduced to as a society and, for some people, this is okay. But to make a final and powerful impression on the hiring manager, break from this new-age society norm of the quick and thoughtless and prepare a thank-you letter on real paper and sign it with a real signature. This small token of appreciation to the company for considering you for the job can be the one thing that tips the scale in your favor. Do not send your thank-you note by

### ◄ JUST GIVE ME THE DAMN JOB!

email and do not sign the letter using an electronic auto signature. It should be your actual signature on a card that you mail by dropping it off in a mail box. Why do you think Donald Rumsfeld, the former Secretary of Defense, took so much heat from the families of fallen soldiers of the Iraq War when he wrote letters to their families with an auto stamped signature? Rumsfeld took the heat because it was perceived by the families of these fallen soldiers that he didn't care enough. I'm sure that Rumsfeld cared a great deal, but the negative perception was ingrained in the minds of families because the auto signature made the communication appear otherwise. The thank-you letter must come across as genuine and heartfelt.

Your thank-you letter should be several paragraphs. You don't want to rehash the interview, but you do want to give the hiring manager one last impression as to who you are and what you are all about. The thank-you letter should make four points:

1. Thank the hiring manager for the interview – *"I want to take this time to personally thank you for interviewing me for the medical assistant position in the trauma ward."*
2. Briefly reflect on one or two key points made during the interview – *"After you explained in detail the fast pace of working in the trauma ward, I am even more excited about the position now than I was before I interviewed."*
3. Restate your interest in the position and sell your theme – *"I do want you to know that I am ready to join your team and look forward to working with you. I am sure that my fifteen years of working in customer service will prove valuable in such a fast paced environment."*
4. Close with a thank-you and contact information – *"Again, thank you for the opportunity and I can be reached at either number listed."*

There is no doubt in my mind that if you apply all of the lessons that we've discussed in this book, you will be at the top of the list for that job of your dreams. Remember,

## CONCLUSION

1. Preparation, preparation, preparation
2. Establish your theme
3. Get a solid night of sleep
4. Dress for success
5. Embrace your positive energy and,
6. NAIL THAT JOB!

I would love to hear from you. Let me know how your interview went. You can reach me at doc44120@yahoo.com. Take care and have a great career!

# Key Points to Remember

1. Most people don't have a clue how to prepare for an interview.
2. Don't leave any doubt that you want the job!
3. Before you can embark upon an adventure, it is first necessary to understand all of the dimensions associated with that adventure. Only then can there be enlightenment. That enlightened experience is necessary to catapult you to the greater understanding of existence and purpose.
4. It's not just about sharing, it's about convincing those who you want to hire you that (1) you are who you say you are and (2) you are more than capable of fulfilling their job expectations.
5. An interview is not a counseling session with your therapist. It's a job interview in which your responses to questions will make or break your career.
6. Job candidates must focus on those activities over which they have control over.
7. The resume got you to the interview. But it can also lose you the job if you aren't able to defend everything that's in it during the actual interview.
8. The interview does not start when you sit down to respond to your first question and nor does it end after you've answered the final question. It started the second you met the receptionist in the lobby and ended when you were safely back in your car driving home.

## JUST GIVE ME THE DAMN JOB!

9. It is important to <u>sell yourself</u>, but also make sure to <u>check yourself</u> so you do not come across like a self-absorbed know-it-all.
10. Don't you dare leave that interview without letting them know that you want the job!
11. The dinner interview has nothing to do with dinner!
12. Remember, your job is to get the job and do so by any ethical means necessary.
13. The first defense that you have against technical glitches is prevention. Know your equipment!
14. You don't want to suppress nervous energy. You want to embrace it and use it to your advantage.
15. Successful hiring managers are tuned in to all signals that the candidate is emanating and they are determining if there is a correlation between what is said and what the other senses are expressing.
16. Before others form an impression about you based on your words, they are forming an impression based on your attire.